A POCKET WITH A HOLE

A Pocket With A Hole

A Birmingham Childhood
of the 1940s and 1950s

by

Brenda Bullock

BREWIN BOOKS

First published by
Brewin Books, Studley, Warwickshire, B80 7LG
in 1995

ISBN 1 85858 080 3

British Library Cataloguing in Publication Data
A Catalogue record for this book is available from the British Library

Typeset in Times by Avon Dataset Ltd, Bidford on Avon, Warks, B50 4JH
Printed in Great Britain by The Heron Press, Kings Norton, Birmingham

For my sister, Kate, who knows what it feels like

Acknowledgements

Line Drawings by Matthew Bullock.

Pictures on pages 40 and 105 kindly lent by Edna Hill.

Wolves Programme and Billy Wright picture (pages 121 and 122) printed by kind permission of Wolverhampton Wanderers Football Club.

CHAPTER 1

The Grove

The Grove, the little road tucked out of sight in a maze of streets in an unfashionable suburb of Birmingham, where I spent the first nine years of my life, is still there. The houses have been done up, of course; double

Stancroft Grove

glazing, new hardwood front doors, paved drives and the like, but the place is essentially the same as it was all those years ago, when it was the centre of my world.

Why it was called a 'grove' only the builders, anxious for a more fashionable image than that given by 'street' or 'road', knew, for there wasn't a tree in sight. It was just a steep, very narrow road, just wide enough for one car to wheeze asthmatically up, as my Gran did, to the top, where it opened out into a small circle, round which was clustered a group of small semi-detached houses, with neat front gardens. The gardens were marked off from the pavement by three-foot high, crenelated walls made from rough concrete cubes, large and grey, all knobbly and uneven, covered by a coating of what looked like coarse sugar, walls which were a common feature of housing estates in the Birmingham of the 1930s. They reminded me of giant, dirty, sugar lumps, all so abrasive to the touch that to brush up against them would leave you with scraped knees and knuckles.

At the top of the narrow entrance road, half way round the circle, on the edge of the pavement stood a symmetrically placed lamp-post, round-headed and arms outstretched, useful for drawing wickets on for the games of cricket we played in the summer, and conveniently placed near enough to the wall of Aunt Doll's house to allow us the adventure of attaching a rope to the arms of the post and launching ourselves at great risk to life and limb from the top of the wall, out over the pavement, where we swung daringly and breathlessly round and round the post until we fell off, either from lack of rope or lack of breath.

The Grove's being on a hill was both a blessing and a curse to the residents. Gran, who, so we were told frequently by Mom in a hushed whisper, suffered from a weak heart, and yet went off cheerfully to work until she was well into her seventies, found this last climb before home a great trial and had to lean on the rough sugar-lump wall half way up the hill to get her breath back, before going the last steps into the circle of houses and home. We children, on the other hand, had hours of amusement putting a board onto a roller skate and hurtling down the steep incline, hair streaming out behind us as we gathered speed and finally clattered into the gutter at the bottom, or skidded straight across the main road to come to a sickening halt up against the kerb stone on the opposite side of the road. Nobody had cars in those days, so there was no danger of our being crushed to death by a car in our helter-skelter journey across the roadway.

2

Ball games were equally hazardous, for if we failed to stop the ball at the top of the hill, chances were that it would roll to the bottom and disappear into the drain that seemed to us to have been deliberately placed just for that.

Many a play session was interrupted by agonised shrieks of "Stop it, Bren!" as the ball soared over my head and began to roll down the steep slope of the Grove, gathering speed as it rushed, lemming-like towards its watery grave, followed by a group of frantic children, moving down the hill with a curious crab-like motion, in a vain attempt to block the ball with an outstretched foot before it vanished into the dark jaws of the drain and was lost, leaving only the recriminations.

"It's your fault, you should have caught it!"

"Well, you threw it too hard."

"Well you throw it anywhere, but I still catch it."

Many a time, wise old ladies would see a group of us glum children, prodding ineffectually with sticks through the bars of the grating over the drain, in a vain attempt to locate the lost ball, and warn us darkly of the dreaded 'fever' that would be bound to claim us if we persisted in spending our time leaning over drains. As far as I remember none of us actually succumbed to 'the fever' from this unhealthy pastime, but the threat hung over us like a spectre, and we never but once got a ball back after it had been swallowed up by the drain. This once was when a cousin, just home from work, took pity on us and levered off the grating in order to fish the ball out from the murky waters beneath. Even then Mom had thrown the retrieved ball straight into the dustbin, afraid of the numerous (of course, unspecified) germs that it no doubt harboured after its dunking in sewer-water. Lesson learnt, we all became expert catchers, or else we'd never have had any games at all, and the sewers would have been blocked by a veritable army of rubber balls!

The circle of six pairs of identical semi-detached houses was home to a fair number of my relations. The houses were small, though my mother, in an unconscious parody of estate agents' jargon, liked to call them grandly 'two parlour types'. The front door gave onto a small square hall, but since no-one ever seemed to use the front door at all, the hall somehow seemed to be overlooked and not really used. Only the rather posh Turners at number 8 insisted on callers using the front door: for the rest of us, neighbours, tradesmen and familiars were all expected to come round the back and use the kitchen door. The kitchen itself was small and narrow, so small in fact that two were definitely a crowd in it. The sole furniture was a large, heavy, crock sink, a gas cooker, a rickety wooden table and a 'dresser' – a wooden cupboard cum drawers affair, where cutlery and crockery were kept. At the end of the room near the back door was the pantry, where the food was kept. Behind this, with the entrance outside, next to the kitchen door, was the coal house, where we had to stand out in the inclement weather to fill our bucket with coal. The back parlour, facing onto the back garden, was usually the living room for the family, the front parlour being kept for best, when visitors came, or when there was an unusually large crowd at Christmas. Upstairs was a tiny bathroom and three bedrooms, the biggest and best being the one at the front of the house, which boasted a rather fine bay window.

Our family didn't have the luxury of all that space because we – my parents, myself and my brother Reggie, lived with my Aunt Doll. We had used to live three doors away, with my Gran and Grandad, but when, with the war on, my father and my uncle had both gone off to fight, we had moved in with my aunt, to help her afford to keep her house going while her husband was away defending freedom in Burma. My mother explained

Gran's house in the 1940s

to us that it was an arrangement 'of convenience', which seemed to me not to be the word to use at all, since, with the passing of time, we became more and more overcrowded and the arrangement offered us no convenience whatever. Even at the beginning it was a tight fit: we had the back parlour, my parents had one bedroom and Reggie and I shared another, leaving my aunt and her young son to have the front parlour and the large front bedroom.

Our houses being marooned at the top of the hill meant that we were a close-knit little community in our circular enclave and this was made more tight by the fact that many of the people were related. Apart from my parents and their children, and Aunt Doll and her family, there were my grandparents and Aunt Doll's in-laws all living within four doors of each other. My unmarried Aunt Maud lived with my grandparents. She was a large, lumpy, angular woman, who my mother sniffily asserted was 'not quite the thing', by which rather odd expression we understood her to be intellectually lacking. She was, however, good-hearted and entirely inoffensive, and got on well with everybody. Aunt Doll lived next door to her mother-in-law, a widow, whose two remaining grown-up children, Mary and Arthur, lived with her. She was a jolly, garrulous woman, who loved a laugh and seemed to fill all available space. Arthur and Mary, frankly neither very bright nor attractive, were doomed never to marry. During their mother's lifetime they were sociable enough, often coming round to Aunt Doll's house for tea and a chat, but after their mother's death they both lost all interest in life and remained like prisoners in their house, reclusive and secretive, living in semi-darkness, since they rarely opened the curtains, in increasing squalor, which made calling upon them a distinctly unsavoury experience, nourished by what food concerned relations cared to send round. Arthur seemed disinclined to venture out, but Mary could on occasions be seen wandering about the area, dressed in a dirty gabardine macintosh of indeterminate colour, a grubby faded blue beret pulled down over her straggly hair.

On the other side of the Grove, opposite Gran's house, lived Lizzie, her half-sister and her family. Gran and Lizzie shared the same father, a fearsome patriarch who lived to be 99, so I was told. I have very vague memories of having seen the venerable gentleman once, but so vague is the recollection that he remains in my mind as being exactly like pictures I've seen since of Bernard Shaw! Lizzie's husband, Sam, was a swarthy, well-built man with a shock of black hair, much reminiscent of a fairground gypsy. Indeed, he boasted that his mother was a gypsy. I found him rather alarming and avoided calling on Aunt Liz when he was at home.

Lizzie's older children were all married. So insular were we that they all seemed to marry very local people. Arthur, the eldest son, married a girl from a few streets away, one of the innumerable daughters of a large Irish family. As she was called Martha, the poor couple had to endure many a tired witticism on their names and many a raucous chorus of the old song:

"Oh, Arthur, what have you done to Martha, Arthur?
Martha's not the same girl now!"

particularly after Arthur, while showing off his swanky new car to us suitably impressed children, drove too fast round the corner leading into the Grove, allowing the badly-closed door to fly open and deposit the unfortunate Martha, red-faced and pride bruised, in the gutter!

The second son, Ronnie, took the principle of marrying local girls to the extreme, marrying the sister of the wife of my father's younger brother. John, the youngest son, confounded tradition by joining the navy, hence the rather faded photograph of the assembled crew on the deck of H.M.S. Ark Royal, which had pride of place on Lizzie's wall, the assembled sailors being no more than anonymous white dots on the deck – but as John was in there somewhere, it was a memento to be treasured. Of the girls, Olive was too old to pay much attention to us, but we played with the younger girls, Pat and Jane.

The only real outsiders in the Grove, with whom we had anything to do, were an old lady who lived at the corner house, and whom we dismissed as being a witch, mainly, it must be admitted, because of her refusal to let us have the ball back if it went onto her garden, and the Turner family who lived next to Aunt Liz and who, feeling themselves to be socially superior to us, didn't really encourage familiarity. They expected you to call at the front door, not come round the back, and they once astonished me when I called asking for change for the gas meter, by saying that they must go upstairs to fetch it. Our families never owned any more money than what they had in their pockets.

We clannishly viewed the people who lived in the road that crossed the bottom of the Grove as being foreigners, and indeed, surprisingly enough, many of them were. My mother spoke disparagingly of them as 'those Welsh people', and viewed them with great suspicion. What on earth a small community of Welsh exiles was doing in a suburb of Birmingham I never discovered, but we never understood their habit of sitting out on the front doorstep in the evening, shawls over shoulders, watching the world go by and chatting in Welsh. After all, front doors, as far as we were concerned, were not for opening. They were kind, humorous people, who never did us any harm, but my mother all her life was apt to declare, a propos of nothing in particular, that she had never liked the Welsh.

The baker, the milkman, and other tradesmen came round to the back door, and if there was no-one at home, they left their wares on the table in the kitchen. No-one ever thought of locking the back door when there was no-one at home. The vans of both baker and milkman were drawn by huge horses, who terrified me. Dogs and cats were familiar creatures: we always had a dog at our heels, usually a cross-breed of indeterminate parentage, but I'd never even seen a cow, and huge dray horses held for me all the terror of an alien species. We used to come out timidly and watch them from a safe distance, as they munched contentedly from their nose-bags as their masters did their rounds. Legend had it that one of these beasts has once seized one of Aunt Lizzie's daughters by the hair, lifted her off the ground and shaken her like a rag doll, until forced to let go of her. No-one could quite remember which of the two horses had been the culprit, or, indeed, who exactly the victim had been, but I, for one, believed the story implicitly and prudently gave both animals a wide berth, partly, I think, because the smell of warm horse, straw and manure, was a foreign odour that I did not recognise.

Apart from the regular calls by the usual tradesmen, we saw very few outsiders in the Grove. One group of callers whose visits were guaranteed to strike superstitious dread into the heart of my grandmother was the gypsies, who called from time to time, peddling pegs, lavender, lucky heather, and the like. My grandmother was sent into paroxysms of mortal terror by their visits: she dreaded having the gypsy's curse put upon her so deeply that she would give them anything they asked for to make them go away. She was a poor woman and couldn't always afford to buy their wares, but she bartered with them so that they wouldn't leave her door without her having had something from them. On one memorable occasion she gave them my grandfather's best (and only) white shirt in exchange for a little white heather. She explained later that she'd felt so sorry for the man as "He didn't even have a shirt to his back" but I don't think Grandad shared her chararitable sentiments when he came to put on his best shirt to go out that weekend. It didn't seem to have been lucky for him, at any rate!

Ours was, for the most part, a cosy and harmonious little community. Even the Welsh people, whom my xenophobic mother distrusted, were good and cheerful neighbours, and life was generally serene enough. Or it would have been had it not been for the family that lived at the corner house at the bottom of the Grove. Their little semi was cold, cheerless, dirty and neglected, which reflected only too well the people who lived there. They were what would be called in later years, a 'problem family'. The father was a brutish bully who beat and starved his wife in equal proportions. My female relations, when they spoke of the family, would say in hissed stage-whispers that the couple weren't even legally married, but as I was too young to have any strong views on the sanctity of the married state, I was more concerned with the pitiful state of the children of the union. We were not rich by any standards: we were, in fact, just poor working class, but these children were something else entirely, and their misery distressed me beyond words. They were ragged, dirty, smelly, visibly undernourished: they had lice and impetigo, and I was as forbidden to play with them in case I succumbed to their many shudder-making ailments. I couldn't have played with them anyway – I couldn't bear to see their misery. I remember once feeling a choking rage when I heard that my Uncle Sam (Aunt Lizzie's husband), who served as the local barber in his spare time, had actually cut the hair of the father of these miserable children, and I never really forgave Sam for what I saw as a fraternisation with the enemy. I only wished he'd cut his throat.

CHAPTER 2

Daily Life

Life during the war was full of privations, shortages, hardship, and 'going without' quickly became an everyday maxim. For me, born a month after the outbreak of the war, of course, it was the only life I had known. Relations talked nostalgically of the luxuries, the halcyon days 'before the war', when the darkened streets were ablaze with light; fruit, a good steak and other mere dreams were commonplace, but this all meant nothing to me. I was born in the blackout: indeed, in one sense, I was born because of the blackout. My mother had been going to the shops in the dark one evening, when she had been startled by a figure jumping out at her from a dark corner. The resulting shock had led to her giving birth to me the following day, a puny child, a month premature and weighing only three and a half pounds. The dark, the lack of basic necessities, the bombing, all the paraphernalia of war, were all the life I knew. I lapped up the stories about the paradise that life had been before the war, of course, but the aftermath of the war came as something of an anticlimax, as these things are wont to do.

When we were walking to the cinema one dark night, my mother pointed out a petrol station on a corner, a typically 1930s building, with a round canopy over the forecourt,with a strange pointed stalk in the middle, rather like an upturned mushroom, and my mother painted such an attractive picture of the pre-war neon lighting running all round the outline of the building, that I longed to see the multi-coloured illumination of the concrete whiteness of the building. When, after the war, a long line of neon tube ran round the white circle of the pointed stalk once again, I must confess to being deeply disappointed. I suppose I'd imagined something more akin to Blackpool illuminations: no doubt deprivation breeds a taste for excess!

I also remember at the beginning of the war being given small round

Gran on her way home from work (1959)

chocolate sweets, with a heavenly honeycomb centre that melted in the mouth. All through the war this taste of paradise stayed with me, but it wasn't until well into the 1950s that I was finally once again transported to bliss by my first taste for many years of what turned out to be Maltesers. They've never tasted so good since, as my memory of them, clung to through all the miseries of the war as a promise of better things to come.

One of the major things we noticed as children during the war was a society almost totally dominated by women. The only man in our lives for most of the war was Grandad, who was too old to be called up. As he worked permanent nights, we never actually saw him all that much, as he was sleeping during the day. Our lives were totally dominated by female influence: Mom, Aunt Doll, Gran, Aunt Lizzie, Aunt Maud, all took care of us, and we slipped in and out of any of the houses as if we lived in them all. All the women, including Gran, worked long hours in the factories, keeping the war effort going. Only Mom stayed at home, to look after the children.

Even after the war all the women worked. Gran worked until she was well over 70, making the long journey every day from home to town, then across town to a road off the Parade, where she worked in a factory making pen-nibs. Very occasionally, Mom took us to Gran's work on a Friday to fetch her. We loved it. We'd be shown round the factory, small and cramped, full of boxes full of shiny silver pen-nibs, which we would pick up and let slip through our fingers back into their box with a metallic tinkle. The workers all seemed to us incredibly old, like Gran; all rough, kindly and tough old ladies, used to the hard life and with a lack of knowledge of the world that astounded even us ignorant children. One old lady greeted the news of the Russian's first satellite that landed on the moon with the dismissive words, "I don't know why it should bother us. After all, it's not our moon they're messing with, is it?" It was quite clear that she believed that each nation had their own moon, just, presumably, as they had their own sun.

Our pockets full of pen-nibs, valuable trophies, given us by the workers, we made off to the Parade, where Gran bought us an ice-cream at Devoti's ice-cream parlour, before we entered another shop, now just half-remembered. The abiding memory is of the smell: a country smell of seeds, which lay in open sacks about the floor. Tools and implements hung from the ceiling of what was like a dark and cluttered cave. I loved it for the strange, unfamiliar smell and for the little paper packets of glassy yellow beads you could buy, which could be threaded on cotton at home to make handsome, clinking necklaces.

During the war life was hard for the women. Not only were the hours of work long, often after sleepless nights spent down in the shelters because of air-raids, but they also had to suffer the shortages, the privations and the curse of the age – queueing. It wasn't too much of a hardship to put up with rationing – at least there was always the consolation, and this was a really unifying force, that everyone else was in the same boat, and fetching chips in a basin because of the newspaper shortage was a novelty rather than an imposition. We soon became inured to the taste of dried egg, which sat like a pale yellow cliff (and just as hard and unpalatable!) on the plate, masquerading as scrambled egg, and to the loathsome 'Pom', the dried potato which was supposed to be brought miraculously to life by the addition of water to become delicious mashed potato, but which, in truth, tasted more like wallpaper paste than anything edible. We got used to minute rations of meat, microscopic pieces of cheese, and blocks of government-issue margarine, an unhealthily bright shade of yellow, which always had my mother reminiscing sentimentally about real butter. I, who had never tasted butter, however, found it hard, come the end of the war, to give up my familiar margarine.

So great was our yearning for something sweet (after all, we never even had fruit), that once, when Mom had managed somehow to acquire a strawberry jelly, we persuaded her not to make it up as a jelly but to cut it into squares for us to eat like sweets. We rolled the big, sweet, squashy, juicy jujus round our mouth, reluctant to swallow them, making their sweetness last as long as possible. It was a taste that stayed with us for days, to be savoured in our memories.

We could stand all this; we could even stand making cakes whose ingredients it was better not to enquire closely into. We made jam with parsnips . . . all this was bearable. What drove everybody crazy, however, was the necessity of wasting hours every day at the end of some queue or other. Even the permitted rations had to be queued for and many long hours were wasted waiting in yet another queue that might, just might, mean a piece of cheese, an orange, or some other fabled luxury. A word on the grapevine that any local shop had anything edible to distribute would lead all the womenfolk to abandon their domestic duties and hurry off to join yet another queue.

I was frequently reminded, although, of course, I didn't remember the incident myself, of the time when my mother had stood for hours in a queue to gain the prize of two fresh eggs, only to find when she finally emerged from another shop that I, who was only a baby, had gleefully cracked them together, leaving two sunny little yolks nestling in the woolly blanket of the pram. I had been delighted with the satisfying mess I'd made: my mother's feelings were less happy! It wasn't all gloom, however. One day Mom had joined her second queue, having got all she could from the grocer. As she waited her turn in the greengrocery queue, Reggie, who was always hungry, began ferreting in Mom's shopping bag to see what he could find to eat. He seized a parcel that seemed promising: a square, heavy thing. Opening the packet revealed a large yellow square. Convinced that this was more cheese than he'd ever seen before, he prepared to take a huge bite from it. My mother's warning: "Don't you dare bite that!" (she knew he'd disobey!) didn't deter him, and he sank his teeth into a block of washing soap! Gales of laughter ran round all the rest of the queue as he spat out his mouthful of soap, blowing bubbles, and red with embarrassment.

Along with food shortages came, of course, shortages of clothes. All clothes were on coupons: no coupons meant no clothes. What clothes were available were generally drab, all the material bearing the familiar 'utility' label. Once, from I know not where, one of my aunts acquired some parachute material – yards of cloth! The only problem was that it was a strange silvery colour, which made me think irresistibly of the barrage balloons that hung above us in the skies. Still, with my mother's admonishments about not looking gift horses in the mouth, I humbly thanked my aunt for underwear made from this precious material, secretly thankful that nobody but me had actually to see it!

We children were clothed mostly thanks to Aunt Doll's talent for knitting. Woollen skirts, sewn on to bib tops made from left-over material, woollen jumpers, school knickers made from scraps of blackout material, comprised my attempts at sartorial elegance, and I really thought I'd got off lightly. That was until my grandmother, obsessed by my being a delicate child who must be kept warm at all costs, bought for me, using her own clothing coupons, I suppose, the most scratchy, irritating, embarrassing and all-envelopping woolly combinations you ever saw. Mom proudly buttoned me into the hideous one-piece garment, short sleeves and legs that reached almost to my knees, reassured that her child would be preserved from the worst rigours of the winter, while I felt like an early Christian martyr in the regulation hair-shirt. After having been driven nearly frantic with itching for a few weeks, I found that successive poundings with the dolly maid during washing at least softened them enough to make them tolerable to wear. Although I hated to admit it, they turned out in the end to be a very welcome ally against the cold in years to come.

Make-do-and-mend was the slogan for all of us in the way of clothes. Reggie wore cut-down trousers and other hand-me-downs from older cousins, and multi-coloured jerseys, fashioned by my aunt from scraps of wool. He looked like Joseph in his coat of many colours, only the ill-fitting grey trousers spoiling the image. I used to watch, fascinated, while my unmarried aunt applied leg make-up and drew a thin line with an eyebrow pencil down the back of each leg, to simulate seams in stockings, before she went out to the cinema or to a dance in the evening. It seemed strangely glamorous to me, but heaven help her if it rained!

Although these days clothes and fashion are subjects of enormous interest to people of all ages, clothes were equally important to us during the war and after, not because we needed to look attractive, but because there was an imperative need to keep warm. A severe fuel shortage just after the war, was followed, in the perverse way that Providence seems to have of working, by the big freeze of 1947. At first, of course, it was all great fun to us children. We loved leaping into massive snowdrifts, getting our wellies full of snow: even going to the shops became something of an adventure. On a piece of waste land with a steep slope that swept down to the pavement, some older boys had made a treat of a slide – three inches thick with ice and a gradient that made it a daunting proposition, even to the bravest. We came across it, Reggie and I, on our way to the shops. To the big boys, to slide down standing up, without falling over and reducing yourself to a figure of ridicule, was a matter of honour. Pete Butcher, the local role-model for all aspiring macho boys, could, naturally, slide down in immaculate style, with ne'er a wobble. The others varied from competent to ludicrous in their attempts. I watched them for a while, all trying, often in vain, to keep both their balance and their dignity, heartily thankful that I was only 8, and a soppy girl to boot, and so had no pride to protect. Thankfully, I folded up the shopping bag that Reggie had given me to hold while he negotiated the slide, sat on it like a mat, and slid safely and exhilaratingly down the monster slide, coming to a skidding halt on the pavement. Was it envy I saw in the boys eyes as I picked up my wet shopping bag and went sedately on my way to the shops?

But, of course, the bitter winter wasn't all fun. Fuel had to be got from somewhere and all too often Reggie and I were the ones deputed to go in search of it. Many a morning we had to brave the freezing darkness at 6 am to push our old pram a couple of miles into Sheldon to a fuel depot. Wrapped up against the cold, Reggie in his knitted balaclava, me in my woollen pixie-hat, tied securely under my chin with strings, with scarves passed crosswise over our chests (to guard against bronchitis) and pinned securely at the back by a large safety pin, our woollen gloves attached to us by strings, for fear that we should lose one, we pushed our old pram to the yard and waited, with a huge number of others, our turn to be served. A man so black with coal that he was hard to see in the semi-darkness would shovel coal onto the scale, then the precious hundredweight of coal (that was all we were allowed), would cascade with a satisfying clatter into our pram, whereupon we would hand over our money and push our burden home again, in time for us to go to school.

What stayed in my mind most vividly about this dawn trek was the bitter memory of one dark morning being on our way to the yard, when people were on their way to work. We were passed by a lady, an office worker I supposed, for she was dressed in a dark costume, who, as she passed us, stared at us in distaste, as if we were beggars and then turned her sneering glance into our pram, black with coal dust and grime. A feeling of shame and blind fury came over me as it dawned on me that this woman, who no doubt felt herself to be far superior to us, was actually expecting as she looked into our pram to see in there a dirty, ill-cared-for baby! Tears of humiliation and rage welled up in my eyes: to think that this woman thought we were those sort of people! Before this, I'd never really felt poor or disadvantaged, but from then onwards, coal fetching, which had once been merely an inconvenience, became a humiliation.

Some days, a buzz on the grapevine that there were logs to be had at Webbs, a wood yard in Yardley, next to the cemetery, would send us and our trusty pram trudging off to wait in yet another queue in the hope of a precious bag of logs. If no logs were to be had, then it was back to the dawn torture of scouring every possible yard for supplies. Desperation often drove us into town at first light, on the first bus, to Adderley Street coal depot to try our luck at buying a bag of coke. Should we be lucky, we half carried, half dragged the large sack, lumpy with the sharp-edged coke, and difficult for small children to handle, to the nearest bus-stop where we waited for a bus whose conductor would take pity on a couple of youngsters and let us on his bus with our unwieldy burden. Often it was a long wait before we found a conductor generous enough to let us on: the rough side of too many tongues was what we generally felt before the warm interior of a bus bore us home again, just in time for school.

Life was hard, yet we never thought to complain. After all, I had never known anything else, and even in the dark days of war, there were bright spots. Children had, of course, very few toys during the war-time, but one Friday night my unmarried Aunt Maud let slip casually that a lady with whom she worked made little bags for girls, in the shapes of animals, and that she had ordered one for me, in the shape of a rabbit. I couldn't believe my luck and quizzed her persistently on just what it would look like, what colour it would be, whether it would have handles and, most importantly, just when this undreamed-of treasure would appear. For the next few weeks I spent Fridays in a positive ferment of tremulous excitement in case this was the day, trying not to get too excited in case it wasn't yet my turn. After what seemed to me to be an age, the Friday came when Aunty pulled from her work bag her sandwich tin, her milk bottle, her packet of tea, and then, triumphantly, just when I was beginning to subside into my chair with disappointment, a black velvet bunny-bag, with long rabbit ears. The soft velvet body was topped by a zip, which when opened revealed a lined interior for me to keep my most precious treasures in. At head and tail was attached a smart black cord which I could slip over my shoulder to carry my bag. What a morale booster it proved to be! I lived for the next few weeks in a rabbit-induced state of euphoria, and spent so much time affectionately stroking my surrogate pet that I wore the velvet on one of his sides quite away.

Morale also received a boost whenever Gran used to say to us in confident tones as we sat on her lap before going off home to bed: "Never mind. One of these days I'll take you to Holt Fleet. You'll like that."

I'd never heard of Holt Fleet: indeed, Reggie and I hadn't ever been out of Birmingham, but to me the name held all the promise of Shangri-La. In a way, I suppose, it was just as well that we never actually had our promised outing with Gran, and Holt Fleet just remained in my memory, a delicious mirage, always just out of reach, for, when, many years later on an outing with my husband in Worcestershire, we passed through the much dreamed-of Holt Fleet, I must confess to a sharp pang of bitter disappointment on finding that all that was there was the large public house on the banks of the placid river that flowed into the distance, before bending out of sight round the tree-lined margins. Then I thought of what fun we would have had by the river if we had actually had our childhood outing and I've gone on calling it Shangi-La ever since.

As the war intensified and the bombing of the Midlands became more heavy and frequent, we all could have done with some little treat to look forward to to make it bearable. We used to sit indoors at night, listening with a choking feeling of dread for the sound of the aeroplanes droning overhead. My mother could tell from the sound of the engines which were ours and which were enemy. Young though I was, I still felt the relief when she, after listening intently as they approached, said reassuringly:
"It's all right: they're ours."

One night we heard with a mounting sense of fear, wave after wave of enemy bombers droning across the skies in the dark above us, but we waited in vain for the sirens to summon us to the shelters. The aeroplanes simply went on and away. We were completely mystified: there had been so many of them. Next morning, my female relations discussed the fact that overnight Coventry had been completely destroyed by air raids. Our salvation, they agreed, had been bought at the expense of some other poor beggars.

I was glad of the nights when the sirens didn't sound; not, as the adults were, because it gave them the rare chance of a good night's sleep before their long working day, but because it meant that I didn't have to go down into Gran's shelter. My aunt's shelter was set into a bank of earth at the bottom of the garden and was entered through an ordinary door, like a shed, but Gran's simply looked from the outside like a grassy mound in the garden. It seemed to me like some subterranean dungeon, approached by some decaying wooden steps, down which I would reluctantly go when forced to do so, clutching my hideous gas-mask, which was called euphemistically a 'Mickey Mouse' mask (presumably to make it more acceptable to children). If this was the aim, however, it was a miserable failure, for it had a dark red, stiff rubber tongue that protruded from the front, which I found quite horrific. We often spent whole nights in the dank darkness of the shelter, family and neighbours, sitting on the wooden slats set round the edge of the shelter, like patients in a doctor's waiting room, our nostrils assailed by the constant smell of damp earth and the close proximity of so many bodies, our feet dragging in water which seeped through the corrugated iron panels and made pools on the floor, unseen in the dim light, but felt all the same.

One night when Birmingham was 'getting a bashing' as all the adults agreed, we sat in the gloom, listening to the frightening sound of bombs dropping, it seemed to me to be nearer and nearer to where we were, and the crack of the anti-aircraft fire, coming from the gun battery in Sheldon. It was a few miles away and yet in the quiet between the whistle and bang of the bombs dropping and the explosions made by the guns firing, we could distinctly hear the officer in charge of the guns shouting his orders for his men to fire. Over many months his voice had offered us a comforting familiarity and reassurance as we huddled in our shelter. It gave the adults much comfort to hear his shouted "Fire!" and hear the guns answer him. They felt that we were at least giving Jerry a taste of his own medicine. They took some bleak satisfaction in thinking that we weren't just victims: we could fight back. Then, this one night, as I dozed fitfully in between the noise of the bombs dropping, I was woken up by an enormous explosion, too close for comfort. As people gathered their scattered wits, we suddenly became aware of the silence – no more shouted orders from the gun battery. As it dawned upon the people that there must have been a direct hit upon the battery, I was astonished to look round in the gloom and find that all the family, huddled in the shelter, had tears running unchecked down their cheeks. I began to cry, too, more out of sympathy for their grief than because I knew what they were crying for. It was only when I was older that I realised that that night they had lost a friend, a disembodied voice that symbolised their resistance to what was happening to them, an ally who struck back at the enemy for them while they remained impotently in their shelter. Life in the shelter after this became even more of an ordeal for all of us, and it took a while for morale to be restored.

Strange as it may seem, the war for us children offered us a benefit that made life so much better than it might have been – it gave us space. The bombing gave us the adventure of exploring bombed sites, and the lack of land development, slowed up by the war, gave us land to play on that would all too soon be swallowed up for housing in the post-war housing boom. Behind Gran's house, coming right up to the end of her back garden, was a big field: not a cultivated field, nor a grassy meadow, but a great expanse of land, full of humps and hollows, wild places, nettles, one big tree, and a whole host of hidey-holes to make every game of hide-and-seek into an adventure. The whole field belonged to us: it wasn't flat enough for sports and it was too wild for adults to take any notice of it, but we children loved it. After the war we dragged old pieces of corrugated iron left over from the shelters over to it, covered over several deep holes with them, camouflaged the tops with grass and brushwood, as we'd seen the adults do to create the shelters where we spent so much of the war, and spent our days in our own secret dens. We felt secure in our territory: we knew every inch of the field. Indeed, in later years, before it was used to build houses on, I could still run across it on the darkest night to visit my Gran, and never miss my footing on the uneven, deeply rutted ground. The only things that could fetch us from our wild playground were hunger, or the sound of one of the adults calling: "Children! It's Dick Barton!"

In a flash our games would be abandoned and we'd all make for the nearest house, arriving breathless indoors before the sound of "The Devil's Gallop", which introduced the adventure serial had died away.

Indeed, it wouldn't be an exaggeration to say that the radio was one of the most important things in our lives, both during the war and after. It took us away from the dreariness of austerity, the rationing that went on for so long after the war, and from the continuing harshness of everyday life. We used to turn off the lights in the evening and sit in the flickering firelight to listen to "Appointment with Fear", a series of frightening mystery plays, introduced by Valentine Dyall, "The Man in Black", and be too scared afterwards to go up to bed! We listened in the holidays to "Music While You Work" and "Workers' Playtime", and took refuge in the humour of programmes which offered something more than a gloomy future. There was, they seemed to say, life after war.

And, indeed, there was. The end of the war brought celebrations to the Grove such as we had never seen. Bunting was made from scraps of material from worn-out clothes, moth-eaten Union Jacks were dragged out from dusty old lofts, we dragged the furniture out into the street and parties were the order of the day. My little cousin sat in his high chair and ate until he nearly burst, and as for us, well, we consumed food in quantities that I for one couldn't ever remember seeing on the table at any one time. And when Aunt Doll's mother-in-law leant out of the front bedroom window to wave and cheer, and promptly lost her false teeth in the bushes below, well, it only added to the jollifications.

In Duncroft Road, which ran along the bottom of the Grove, a huge bonfire was lit that completely blocked the road to traffic and we went down there to join in their celebrations too. Potatoes were baked in the fire and handed out to all comers. The spirit of togetherness that had seen us successfully through the war spilled over into the celebrations and I felt almost bewildered by the sense of release of tension, of relief, of sheer elation that seemed to surge through everybody. It was a feeling of shared joy, of closeness between neighbours that I have never experienced since.

That is not to say that the community spirit faded away as soon as the war ended: it didn't. The people, after years of deprivation, of making-do, of suffering, wanted to go out and enjoy themselves, and many Community Associations were set up to create a social life for the people. The prime movers in our local association were a couple who lived in a neat semi near the shops, a house called mysteriously "Chez Nous", which, in my childish ignorance I assumed must be some foreign language for "Chest Nuts", although I couldn't for the life of me think why anyone would want to call a house after such a patently uninteresting thing!

The main events which I remember our association organising were shows, put on in the hall of the school, in which every local person was encouraged to come and perform their 'party piece'. Girls got together to perform cheerful and energetic dance routines, and farcical sketches were performed by the adults, with men dressed as schoolchildren, coming out with such execrable jokes as: "I'm not a girl and I'm not a boy – I'm a mixed infant!" which we all thought were terribly funny! Kenneth Upton, who had a pure treble singing voice entertained us with the latest hit tunes, among them, I remember, "I don't see me in your eyes any more". The shows were always very well attended; after such an awful time, we were all determined to be amused and enjoy ourselves. Such gatherings, and the feeling of solidarity and sheer high-spirits that the end of the war had engendered in us went on long after the war and many local social clubs

Buster enjoying the V.E. day party

formed in this way lingered until well into the 1950s. Ours I remember only until about 1949, when its activities seemed to die, and we shifted our attention to the cinema for our enjoyment, spending many a Saturday night in a long queue that snaked all round the building, before we could get in to see our chosen film.

When the war finally ended, only two soldiers remained to return to the Grove. One was my Uncle Reg, Aunt Doll's husband, who had been away for several years fighting in Burma. I only remember him coming home on leave once. He had turned up totally unexpectedly one night, amid much excitement, and he'd come into our bedroom to show us his rifle, and a few mementoes of Burma. Then, as if it had all been a dream, he'd been spirited away again, not to return until 1945. A neighbour's son, Clarence, was also due to return. My father, who had served with the Marines, had been discharged from the forces during the war on medical grounds, and had been obliged to spend the rest of the war doing his bit as a Captain in the Home Guard. We prepared for the homecoming of our two soldiers by making home-made banners, bearing the legends, "Welcome home, Reg" and "Good show, Clarence", which we attached to the front of their respective houses. When they arrived, it was to a hero's welcome, and to another party, and the feeling of pride and well-being lasted longer than the banners which hung for several weeks under the bedroom windows, bedraggled and limp.

With the war finally over, life became better. I don't suppose the adults noticed much difference, actually, since rationing, shortages and the general misery lasted for several years after the war, but for Reggie and me weekends became times of high excitement. We were old enough by this time to go into town on a Saturday morning, unsupervised, and spend our pocket money, the few pennies that Gran and our parents gave us from their earnings, and which we could spend on anything we liked.

We walked to the bus-stop – by this time the bus service had been extended from the Yew Tree, Yardley, to quite near to where we lived, so we could pay our one and a half pence fare, climb up to the top deck, and travel in style to the centre of Birmingham. Our first port of call on arrival was always Lewis's, the big department store, which boasted a wonderful new toy – escalators. We found them thrilling, and our first amusement was to travel on any escalator we could, riding up and down, trying, as a variation on a theme, to run down the 'up' staircase, thoroughly entertaining ourselves and infuriating the thronging shoppers, until some spoil-sport of an official would tell us to clear off and cordially invite us never to return. Then we'd go up and down the staircases, looking over the banisters from the dizzy heights of the sixth floor, between the gold-coloured metal handrails, right down to the ground floor. I dreamt of sliding down the banisters from top to bottom, but was disgruntled to find that some busy-body, afraid of having the deaths of a multitude of children put to the charge of Lewis's, had put large, uncomfortable bumps on the rail to discourage daredevils such as myself from killing themselves in spectacular style.

We found it very exciting when Lewis's opened their roof garden, where we could walk round the flower beds and then lean daringly out over the balustrades to view the panorama of the city roof-scape and point out to each other the ants and caterpillars down below, which were the people and traffic. Then we would make our way to Pets' Corner, where children were actually encouraged to handle puppies, kittens, rabbits and hamsters. One Saturday, enchanted by the pink eyes and sinuous tails of the white mice, Reggie bought a couple, which he carried home in the pocket of his jacket. We thought them wonderful, so we were totally unprepared for the reception they got when we got them home. Its being Saturday morning, all the female relations were gathered in Gran's back parlour, drinking tea and talking over the events of the week, when we arrived home. As Reggie drew from his pocket our lovely mice, with their twitching noses and bushy whiskers we found, to our utter astonishment, that gasps of fear, high-pitched shrieks and angry cries rose up from all sides. Above the confused babble of voices came Mom's: "Get them out of here!" and two rather confused children, plus two somewhat disconcerted mice, found themselves outside, wondering what all the fuss was about. The mouse owning never really recovered from this unfortunate start: Mom was terrified of them, and never really came to terms with having them under her roof. One morning, Reggie and I came down to breakfast to be greeted by the tragic news that overnight our mice had escaped from their cage and could not be found. In our hearts we knew they would never be found: and they weren't. To this day I don't know what Mom did with them.

After this educational experience, followed by the day we bought from Lewis's food hall some exotic cheese that Mom denounced as 'foreign muck' and promptly consigned to the dustbin, we gave Lewis's a miss for a while and concentrated our efforts on the delights of the Rag Market. Right at the bottom of the Bull Ring, the narrow street that snaked upwards steeply until it opened out into the ring of its name, where stood the beautiful church of St Martin, stood the splendid Victorian Gothic ironwork of the market hall, which held a veritable Aladdin's cave of fascinating objects. First we made for the home-made sweet stall, drawn inevitably by the smell. There we could choose from fishes, long, thin, of delicate colours, with sugar eyes and white sugar stripes; sticky brown troach drops; pastel pink pear drops; acid drops that brought tears to my eyes and made my tongue sore for days afterwards; lumps of dark, sticky toffee that gave us lockjaw and played havoc with our teeth.

We used to spend hours searching out the untold delights of a million objects strange and rare, useful and useless, which cluttered up the many stalls, and we ferreted about for hours without spending more than a shilling. We bought a wide variety of breathtaking bargains: a handbell, that in later years could be painted in partisan colours and taken to football matches; six teaspoons which we proudly presented to Mom (and if she noticed that they were all stamped "F.W.Woolworth", then she was too diplomatic to point it out to us!). We almost bought a Crimean War medal once, but Reggie decreed that at a shilling it was too expensive and I was obliged to relinquish it and opt for something cheaper, but far less interesting than a real war medal.

After spending our time and money in the Rag Market, we always made our way up the Bull Ring. As we climbed the hill, the smell from the fruit stalls which lined both sides of the narrow street wafted towards us and made us hungry. We used to buy an apple for a penny each and eat them as we made our way to a dusty open space where we could stop to watch itinerant performers going through their routines. Our favourite was the escapologist, who would be trussed up in heavy (and not very clean-looking) sacks by a partner, who would then securely chain and padlock him in, leaving him lying in a seemingly helpless heap on the dusty ground. The whole thing worried me: I feared he'd suffocate and I used to wait in a fever of anxiety, even forgetting to bite my apple, while he writhed and kicked in his sack, sending clouds of dust into the air as he struggled to free himself. Then, just as I was beginning to think my worst fears were about to be realised, he always freed himself, and sat dishevelled but triumphant, holding aloft in triumph the chains that had bound him seemingly so securely. Before the crowd could disperse, the partner would pass swiftly among us, and I used to put in a penny as a pledge of the man's future survival. Reggie wouldn't pay, because he denounced the whole show as a cheat, simply because he couldn't fathom out how it was done, I supposed. I don't know to this day if the whole thing was just a trick, but I thought my money well spent, even if the whole thing was a never-ending source of worry to my timid nature.

As we reached the top of the street, where it opened out into the square, we always made for the stall where they sold live day-old chicks. I really loved to handle the fragile, soft little bodies and see their tiny beaks open to emit a plaintive 'cheep', and I cherished an ambition to own some of them. Actually, my dream turned into a nightmare, for we once bought home a box containing half a dozen adorable chicks to my Gran and mother, who set about the business of rearing fowls. Grandad made a little run for them in the garden and our fluffy little chicks soon grew into squawking hens. Then, one fateful morning, we got up to the ominous sound of silence: no vigorous squawking from our hens. Investigation revealed that all that remained of our fine chickens were a few feathers and some gruesome disembodied feet – the prey, we supposed, of some hungry fox.

We didn't entirely give up the idea of rearing fowls, however, for we once returned from town with a duckling (Christened with a deplorable lack of originality, 'Donald'), whom we kept in the house, for fear of his suffering the same fate as the unfortunate chickens. What we would have done with the poor creature had he grown to maturity, was never clear. We were, however, spared such thorny problems by his catching a chill and dying, after which we finally admitted defeat and gave up trying to rear livestock.

When we rode back from town with our purchases, we always went up on the top deck of the bus, from which vantage point we could see all manner of interesting things. We could see over the fence into the sanitorium, where the tuberculosis patients spent years trying to overcome the disease that was the curse of the age. We could see them lying in their beds, out in the open air on fine days, and we'd wave to them and feel sorry for their incarceration in hospital. It was to be many years before the sanitorium became simply East Birmingham Chest Hospital, and the sight of skeletal figures wasting away before our eyes was a thing of the past.

When the bus stopped at the Yew Tree pub in Yardley, we could see over the fence into the garden behind the pub and I was amazed to see grown men indulging in what seemed to me to be a remarkably childish game. It seemed to be a game of marbles, with big black marbles of a size more fitting to adults. They seemed to be made of iron, not glass, and the men bowled them with great accuracy along a lawn as smooth as a carpet. As the bus waited at the stop, I used to try to work out the rules of this fascinating and mysterious game, but I never could. Years later, of course, I learnt that they'd been playing bowls: I was secretly rather disappointed, for I rather liked the idea of adults playing a secret game, cut off from prying eyes, behind a screening wall!

CHAPTER 3

Doctors and Hospitals

I had been a premature baby, weighing only three and a half pounds, and in the days before incubators and modern medical techniques this was a great problem. Indeed, such was the prognosis of my survival chances that, after being wrapped in cotton wool for a week or so, I was allowed out of hospital as soon as I weighed four pounds, and my mother was sent home with me with the cheerful opinion: "You will never rear this child," ringing in her ears. I was put into doll's clothes, which swamped my puny body, and my mother was so afraid of breaking my match-stick limbs when she bathed me that she left this particular task to my grandmother. I was a great expense to my family, for, being premature, I had to have special babymilk, "Allenbury's", and had to be fed with tiresome frequency.

Not surprisingly, given my unpromising beginnings, I was a fairly sickly child, another source of expense for my family, since the National Health Service had not yet come into being, and all consultations with a doctor had to be paid for. Doctors, in those days, were viewed with a respect bordering on awe, for not only did they inhabit large, posh houses, but they both diagnosed your illness and made up the required medicine in their pharmacy before you went home after a consultation.

Our doctor, Dr. Kalra, was remarkable in being Indian, at a time when a coloured skin was a rarity. My grandmother had gone to him as a young woman, when Dr. Kalra had first set up his practice in Birmingham, and she remained his patient until both of them were well into their eighties. He lived in a large detached house some way from our house, a long walk, especially if you weren't feeling very well. I used to be nervous of calling on him: the large oak door and bell pull, (we only had knockers on our doors), I found quite intimidating, and the elegant hall which doubled as a waiting room, with its polished parquet floor, was luxury at which I could only wonder. Sometimes his dog, a large handsome collie, called Boy, would come in and we could play with him while we waited our turn to see the doctor. Actually, looking back, visits to the doctor were more valuable for reassurance than for treatment, since the range of medicines available was pitifully small. The usual prescription if you were an adult seemed to be a large bottle of dark brown medicine, which tasted revolting, (on the principle, I suppose, that if it didn't taste nasty it couldn't do you any good), and a small bottle of medicine of an unnatural pink if you were a child, both with corks shoved roughly into the top and bearing a label that announced grandly that contained within was "The Mixture". My mother swore none of it was any good and, indeed, the row of almost full bottles of the stuff that gathered dust on the top shelf of the pantry bore witness to her lack of confidence in its healing powers.

Actually, people didn't go to the doctor's all that much: they couldn't afford to. They more often than not put their trust in patent medicines and traditional remedies, mixed with old wives' tales. Bad chests were always treated with camphorated oil, which resided in the hearth near the fire, warming gently until bedtime, when Mom would rub a generous handful over our chests before sending us to bed with strict instructions to breathe deeply and let the camphor vapour do its good work of restoring us to health. Gran always swore by goose grease, which she asserted would shake off even the most stubborn bronchitis. She once proudly showed us a bottle of the stuff, lovingly collected from some unfortunate dinner of Christmas past, solid in its bottle like dripping. Fortunately for us, however, geese were hard to come by during the war and we never actually had to endure the wonderful treatment.

Splinters were treated by the magic Blackjack ointment; black, glutinous and miraculous in its effects. A dollop of this, dug from its round, waxed cardboard drum and applied to even the deepest splinter would be guaranteed to deliver it up by the next morning. Swellings on fingers could be relieved by the application of a bread poultice. Boil the bread, squeeze out the excess water, then wrap your hot bread in an old rag and apply it to the affected part. It didn't cure anything, I suppose, but it offered a little welcome relief from the pain of whitlows and septic fingers, before the antibiotics came along to cure them from within.

What a picture we must have presented to the curious beholder when we were ill! We lay there in bed, as slippery as eels with our coating of camphorated oil, the hideous taste of Famel cough syrup in our mouths, tucked up with a hot brick, warmed in the hearth all evening and then wrapped in an old cloth and slipped beneath the sheets to do duty as a hot water bottle. Years later, Dad, who was a metal spinner, made us real hot water bottles; large, flying-saucer shaped copper receptacles which provided blissful warmth on a cold night, for they retained their warmth almost until morning.

Home-made remedies notwithstanding, I had much reason to be grateful for the philanthropic nature of Dr. Kalra, for when I was less than two years old I acquired, as the result of a bout of chickenpox, caught from Reggie, an ear infection, and had to be admitted to hospital. Several months later I emerged from hospital, ostensibly cured, only for the infection to reappear in a most virulent form, no more than a few days after my return home. Back to the Children's Hospital I went, my mother and Reggie in tow.

My mother, who was a woman of remarkable obstinacy and forthrightness, flatly refused to allow me to be admitted to the hospital, declaring that if the aim was to kill me, she could do that quite easily herself at home, thank you very much. I was most seriously ill, as the doctor patiently explained to my mother, but she was adamant. If they had kept me there for months without being able to cure me, what chance was there of their being able to do so now? For much of the day my mother, and my increasingly tired and hungry brother, sat in the waiting room, to 'think over the position' , but my mother firmly refused to alter her opinion. I was not going to be left there. Finally, when my grandmother at home was so worried about what could have happened to us all that she was tempted to call the police, a compromise was reached. My mother was persuaded to take another long bus journey across town to Selly Oak hospital, so that I might be admitted there. So off we went, my mother still muttering that she'd take me there, but that didn't necessarily mean that she'd leave me there, either, but, finally, I was admitted to Selly Oak as an emergency case, with the promise that I should be the first patient that the famous Mr Reading would see when he did his rounds the next morning. Early the next morning, my mother was startled to answer a knock at the door and to find a policeman there, come to inform her that Mr Reading was operating on me that very morning and that my parents could visit me that afternoon. So began a childhood spent in hospital, constantly having my life saved by Mr Reading, who came to look upon me as his child, as I looked upon hospital as 'home'.

The curse of 'mastoiditis', the dreaded ear infection that plagued my childhood, before the advent of the wonder-drugs, the anti-biotics, followed me for years, each infection having as its inevitable corollary yet another trip across town to the hospital, another operation and another long stay in hospital. Winter, of course, was always the worst time, for it was the time for colds which, in me, always led to another ear infection. Often, in dead of night, Dad would cycle over to Dr. Kalra's home; the doctor, (clad, so I was assured, in silk pyjamas), would put his head out of the bedroom window, and then prepare to visit me. I always longed to see the fabled silk pyjamas but, of course, I never did! Before Dad had got home on his bicycle, the doctor would be at our house, and in spite of the vast inconvenience we caused him, he very often refused any payment for his services.

A great deal of my early years were spent lying on the sofa in Gran's back parlour, covered up by my Grandad's overcoat, half-dozing, half-listening to the hum of conversation going on around me, counting the baskets of flowers on the wallpaper. Grandad used to wallpaper the parlour every year, but he was an impatient man and if, by some accident, a piece of wallpaper somehow got itself put on upside down (and one usually did!), well, that's how it stayed, and I used to contemplate at great length the gravity-defying flowers above my head.

As I lay on the sofa, I knew that in the kitchen on the stove was boiling the next instalment of my torture – the kaolin for my next poultice. The tin of kaolin clay was put into a saucepan of boiling water and heated until the clay was developed into a scalding mud. This was spread on an old piece of cloth, folded over, and then applied to my ear. The kaolin sandwich was excruciatingly hot and I wondered frequently whether burns to the ear and face were a fair price to pay for the temporary relief from ear-ache that the fierce heat sometimes brought. If the pain became too much to bear, to take my mind off it, Gran would take me onto her lap and sing to me:

"I leave the sunshine to the flowers,
I leave the springtime to the trees.
And to the old folks I leave a memory
Of a baby upon their knees . . ."

and I would drift off to sleep for a while.

Sometimes the heat from the poultice would burst the abcess in my ear, causing an evil-smelling discharge that matted my hair and made me even more uncomfortable, but more often than not the pain merely heralded another long trip on the Outer Circle bus to the hospital, and yet another operation.

It was wartime and, of course, the general shortages were also felt in the hospitals. The ward I stayed in had beds all round the edge of the room, a long table down the centre of the ward being used for us to take our meals at. At one point in the war, however, I was for a time sent away from the bombing in Birmingham to a hospital in Malvern, where the over-crowding was so acute that we had beds all down the centre of the room as well as packed closely together all round the edge. I hated my stay in Malvern because I couldn't have any visitors. Indeed, our parents were told that they would receive a post-card every week to inform them of our progress, but my mother remembers that she didn't receive any news of me for weeks on end. Finally, when she came to take me home, I still remember the feeling of hurt and despair as she walked straight past my bed: I had grown up so much during my absence from home that she didn't recognise me.

Daily life in the hospital followed a strict routine. At six o'clock in the morning, even in the coldest weather, could be seen a line of little children standing in front of a row of small white sinks, set into a tiled wall at child height, cleaning their teeth and gargling with a liquid of lurid red colour. The more expert spat it out with speed and precision, the youngest swallowed it and choked on the bitter antiseptic taste. That chore over, we would all troop back to our beds to await the next ritual of the morning – the administering of the health-giving cod liver oil and malt. This magic substance was doled out by Sister, accompanied by two nurses who handed her a clean spoon for each child. Sister carried the large jar of pale brown sludge, into which she dug with a spoon, one spoonful for each child. I really rather liked the sweet, malty taste, which successfully disguised the fishy taste of the cod liver oil, but, being a rather nervous child, I nevertheless lived in fear of the ritual. The trouble was that the consistency of the mixture tended to vary from day to day, from hard to virtually liquid. If it was hard, there was no problem: it could be bitten off the spoon like toffee. But if it was all runny, then however wide I opened my mouth and put out my tongue to catch it, more often than not it would run in sticky streaks down the front of my nightie. Then Sister would be cross and the other children would jeer at me for being a baby. I hated that, and much nervous energy was wasted worrying about the dreaded cod liver oil and malt.

With the early chores over, and the Friday morning visits from the consultants out of the way, we found filling up the long days quite difficult. There were no school lessons provided for children in hospital in those days: I used to miss school for months on end, and the war meant that there were very few toys for us to play with. The girls often helped the nurses with their chores: I soon became expert at doing hospital corners in blankets, and sometimes we helped to amuse those children too sick to leave their beds. I was soon up and about after my operations, wearing my bandages like a turban about my head, which covered up the fact that much of my hair had been shaved off for the operation.

The active children soon put their minds to finding games to play that didn't need much equipment. The great favourite was "Jack, Jack, may I cross your golden river?" This was a fine chasing game, in which anyone who did not have the colour specified by "Jack" as necessary for crossing the river, had to try to get across while Jack tried to prevent him and so eliminate him from the game. The only drawback was that all of us wore nighties that were either pale yellow or pale blue, which meant that if Jack specified any other colour, a most unseemly melee would ensue, quarrels would break out, blows would be exchanged, and then the nurses, tired of our antics, would order us back to bed until some more civilised pastime could be devised.

The routine became even more boring to us since we had so few visitors to help pass the time. Visitors were allowed for an hour only twice a week, on Sunday afternoon from 2–3 and on Wednesday afternoon from 2–3pm. It was strictly only two visitors at a time, and so, I and so many children like me, grew up seeing their mother only twice a week for an hour and other relatives on a shift system: mother and father for half an hour, then aunty and grandmother for half an hour. Yet, I suppose, if anyone had thought to point out that children need to be kept in regular contact with parents and family, they would have been severely reminded that during a war nothing is normal for anyone.

Actually, as a chronically sick child, I always felt rather special, for not only did my family and friends go to great lengths to see that I had presents at birthday and Christmas, but also local tradespeople used to save little extras for me. I remember my poor mother traipsing across town in a rainstorm to bring me a birthday cake for my fifth birthday, a cake made specially for me by the mother of an aunt (though heaven knows what went into it!). Being in hospital also meant that in spite of rationing we always got the best of what food was available. We always had a quarter of an orange or a quarter of an apple to finish off our meals, at a time when fresh fruit to most people outside was nothing more than a dim and distant memory.

All food brought in by parents was collected by nurses during the visiting periods, to be shared out equally between all the children. At least that was the principle: in practice we always tried to wolf as much as possible before the nurse got round to us to collect the precious food for the common good. Once, my mother, from heaven knows where, had managed to obtain for me a large bag of shelled peanuts. The sight of such a feast was too much for my rather undeveloped sense of community spirit, and I grabbed two huge handfuls of them, stuffing my mouth most disgustingly full before the nurse could come and rescue the rest! Surprisingly, in view of this obvious selfishness, we always managed to eat rather well, and even the horrible breakfast porridge was made palatable to me by its being served in a dish which had a coloured picture of the cat and the fiddle, from the nursery rhyme, on the bottom of the dish. Coloured crockery, especially that with actual pictures on it, was a real rarity during the war, and I always made a point of finishing my porridge, just so I could see the lovely coloured picture on the bottom of the dish.

I was always in hospital for Christmas, and everyone went out of their way to see that we had a good time. On Christmas Eve we were tucked up in bed, with the time-honoured exhortation to go to sleep quickly or else Father Christmas would not come to us. As we skulked under the bedclothes, trying to look like sleeping angels, yet too excited to sleep, the nurses, dressed in their scarlet cloaks, carrying glowing lanterns on poles, would come into the ward, in a glorious festive show, singing carols to us, while we lay in bed, half wondering if we were dreaming.

One year, the nurses had been hard at work in their spare time, fashioning for us cheeky little rabbits made from brightly coloured scraps of felt, and it was these creatures whom we first saw on waking up on

Christmas morning, peeping saucily at us from the top of our stockings, hung over the bedrail. They were the most colourful things we'd seen throughout the whole war, and we were all delighted with them. But, with the perversity of children, I preferred the blue and red one of the child in the next bed to me, to the blue and white one I had received, and duly arranged a discreet swap when no-one was looking!

On Christmas morning we were all assembled to go round the adult wards to act out the nativity story for the adult patients, who were also away from their loved ones at Christmas. A lucky girl was chosen to be Mary, and the much-coveted Christ-child doll was put into her arms; (most of us hadn't got dolls, since they weren't available during the war). We all longed to hold the doll, but only one girl could be Mary, and it never seemed to be my turn. The rest of us, sporting wings of hospital gauze, were transformed into attendant angels. All round the wards we went, enacting out the ancient story and singing "Silent Night" in our childish trebles, charming our captive audience with our sweetness. And if the angels' wings were sometimes set askew , and Mary was being kicked ferociously from behind by a jealous rival during the singing of the carols, no-one was any the wiser!

We saw very little, really, of adults, but one particular encounter stuck in my mind. I was going home that day and was very excited. Once I was in my outdoor clothes, waiting for my mother to come to fetch me, a nurse told me she'd take me to see someone before I went home. Mystified, I followed her into a little side ward, off the main ward. In the bed lay an old lady, who seemed to me to be hundreds of years old. She was so thin: nothing more than wrinkled brown skin stretched over bone. To be truthful, I was more than a little afraid of this human skeleton, but I obeyed the nurse's exhortation to approach the bed and speak to the lady. She looked kindly at me and spoke a few words, while I stood in an unnaturally starched posture, longing to be allowed out. After what seemed to me to be a long time, but which could only have been a couple of minutes, the old lady reached a skinny hand out towards me and offered me an orange. I'd never had a whole orange before, and was impressed enough to thank the lady politely before being shown out of the room again by a nurse. I still have no idea who she was: from her physical state it would seem that she was dying of tuberculosis. She wasn't there when I next went into hospital, so perhaps I was her last link with life and youth before her death. I can't see an orange now without thinking of that pitiful figure and wishing that I'd been old enough to have the presence of mind to have been more caring and sympathetic to her.

Out I went from my close encounter with near death into the open air, after months of living indoors, in the confined space of the ward. I walked along the streets, holding my mother's hand, looking in amazement at the houses, with their fire buckets outside the front doors, one bucket of water, one of sand; at the buses, the people, the ordinary things of life that I had forgotten while in hospital. The only consolation to me was that, if I had missed normal, ordinary life, I'd also missed the horrid trips down into the dungeon of Gran's shelter.

During the 1940s came the great medical breakthrough that was to transform medical treatment for ever – anti-biotics. Penicillin had been used on the troops during the war, but they were not used for civilians until after the war was over. When, just after the war, I went down with another ear infection, Mr Reading, knowing that another operation would lead me to be partially deaf in one ear, decided to use the new wonder-drug on me, to save my hearing. I was to receive the famous M & B drug. Already the area behind my left ear looked as raw as meat in a butcher's shop and there didn't seem to be anywhere else for an incision to be made, so I was to be the guinea pig for the new treatment. My abiding memory is of tablets that seemed to me to be as large as horse pills and which I had great difficulty in swallowing, but which, I was told, I was a very lucky girl to be able to have. Sad to say, the wonder pills failed to work on my advanced case and so, for the last time, I was again admitted to hospital for the operation that would make me partially deaf in one ear. As happy chance would have it, the Sister on my ward when I had my last ear operation was the very lady who had been Sister on the ward when I'd had my first operation as a toddler, and I was spoilt rotten! I was given everything I wanted to play with, allowed to play with the much coveted box of dominoes whenever I liked, and was cosseted and cared for in such a way as made even the familiar pain, the bandages, the hospital routine, the peculiar feeling on the scalp as the hair was shaved off, seem almost fun. When I left my surrogate parent, the tiny Mr Reading, who had to stand on tiptoe to answer the wall-mounted 'phone, and his enormous assistant, who was six feet three and had hands like coal-shovels, I have to admit to tears. It was like a bereavement for me; I would never again spend months of my life at a stretch in this hospital in which I had spent so many of my formative years.

CHAPTER 4

Primary School

My attendance at school was, with all my stays in hospital, very fitful. Indeed, I remember very little about being in the infants' part of the school. When Reggie had started at the school before the war, it had been no more than a temporary wooden hut, with just a few pupils, but by the time I started there it was a smart, single-storey building, surrounded by an asphalt playground and stout iron railings, to keep the children from wandering out into the road. The infants' part of the school was on the far side of the building, well away from the road, and the junior school overlooked the road.

The Headmistress of the infant school was a kindly, if severe looking lady, whom we rarely saw, but to whom we referred in whispers as "Miss Dark". This seemed to me to be an entirely appropriate name for a lady who always wore sombre clothes and who inhabited a gloomy study on the side of the building where the sun never reached, furnished with chairs and a desk of dark wood which never got a chance to shine. In fact, in later life,

Cockshut Hill Junior School

I learnt that the lady had actually been called "Miss Stark". Not that it mattered, really, for on the few occasions we ever met her, we simply addressed her respectfully as "Miss", and so our mistake was never discovered.

The infant school teachers were all women, usually spinsters of advanced age; at least, we thought them ancient. I lived in fear of having to go into Miss Avery's class, as one of Aunt Lizzie's daughters had had to do, and I dreaded the prospect, for I was in mortal fear of her. She had black, wild hair, a profile reminiscent of the witches we saw in fairy-story books, and she had a temper that was the stuff of legends. As it happened, I needn't have worried: I was hardly at infant school long enough to be in anyone's class for more than a few weeks. Thus was I spared many a rap over the knuckles with a ruler, as a warning against committing even the most minor of misdemeanours.

The chief subjects taught in the infant school were the traditional reading, writing and arithmetic. Reading was taught with the aid of large books which retailed the adventures of animals on a farm. The farmer, Old Lob, cared for his animals: Mr Dan, the sheepdog; Mrs Cuddy, the cow; Willy, the pig and Mary, the bad chick. It seems to me now to have been a singularly inappropriate book to use with poor city children, most of whom had never even seen a cow, but I loved to read about the adventures of the animals, particularly those of the naughty animals. I loved reading about Willy the pig rolling in the soot in the yard, and I still remember the picture of him, all black and dirty, with the caption underneath reading "Bad Willy"!

A great deal of time seemed to be spent copying out poems into our best writing books, and reciting our multiplication tables, so I was more than grateful that my frequent absences from school spared me from such boring pastimes.

The only relief from the classroom came in the form of physical training periods, which took place in the playground, weather permitting. My Gran had, during the war, had a Scottish lodger, a certain Annie Mcleod, come down to give a hand in the factories in the war effort, and this kind lady had made for me a pair of school gym knickers out of a piece of blackout material, so at least I could look the part. In truth, the knickers were my only concession to the ideal of a healthy mind in a healthy body, for I hated P.T. lessons. The physical jerks, with much arm waving and jumping about in unison exhausted me, and 'apparatus time' was little better. The 'apparatus' in question, thanks to the austerity of wartime, consisted of a few saggy bean-bags and a collection of wooden hoops. The hoops were quite fun, for they could at least be trundled down the sloping playground, but the bean-bags were a great disappointment. They simply flopped limply onto the ground when dropped, looking as exhausted as I usually felt. Once, quite by accident, for I was too timid to do anything naughty on purpose, I threw one of the bean-bags over the fence into someone's back garden, which gave onto the school yard, and lived in a slough of utter misery and guilt for weeks afterwards, terrified that my reckless loss of the precious school equipment would be discovered and punished.

Religious education was a subject much favoured in the infant school, and, apart from morning assembly, we also had to say a short prayer before we went home for the day at 3.30pm. We put our chairs up on the desks, to make it easier for the cleaners to clean the room later, then stood before the desks, hands together and eyes closed, while the teacher said a prayer. Reggie had once asked the teacher how she knew his eyes weren't closed if she was obeying her own instruction, and was soundly smacked for his impertinence! Final prayer said, dutiful 'Amens' repeated, we were then let out of school.

Should it be raining when we went out, as a great concession, parents would be allowed into the porch to help us put on wellies and coats. Generally speaking, parents were not welcome inside the hallowed portals of the school. Their world and that of school met but rarely. There were no such things as parent/staff meetings: indeed, it never entered anyone's head that parents had anything to do with the education of their children – that was for the experts. It was to be many years before parents were considered to have anything to offer to the life of their children's school or indeed anything to offer to their children's education.

Much of my infant school time was just a blur – merely a few snapshots of the few times I actually attended. However, once we transferred to the junior school at the age of 7 my attendance became much more regular, and my memories are consequently much more vivid. I hated school. I was so late in coming to formal education that I never really settled to it. I was nervous of the children, who'd all been together in school from the age of 5 and who therefore saw me as an outsider; and I was frankly terrified of the teachers. I lived in constant dread of doing something wrong. School routine was such a novelty to me that I was quite bewildered for much of the time, and the Headmistress seemed to have been put on this earth with the sole intention of being a torment to me. The formidable Miss Goddard resembled a cross between a sorceress and an imperious queen. Her word was law, to both staff and pupils alike. She allied a most uncertain temper to an air of invincible superiority. Her posh Cambridge accent was thick enough to be cut with a knife, and we were bound to come into constant ridicule whenever we opened our mouths and revealed our flat Birmingham accents. She was a strikingly handsome woman, (reputed to have been a great beauty in her youth), with a mane of jet black hair, invariably set into neat, symmetrical black sausage curls. Never was a hair out of place; indeed, it was rumoured by the more naughty children that she took it off at night and hung it over the bedrail, so that she could don it, all lustrous perfection, the next morning. She swept regally about the school during lesson time, causing consternation wherever she went, dropping unexpectedly into classes and reducing teachers and pupils alike to quivering jellies.

I was unfortunate enough to have what was considered a good speaking voice , so I was always forced to be in school plays. Not only was this a

The class of 1948, Cockshut Hill Juniors

sore trial to my timid nature, but it also meant that I had to suffer the ordeal of Miss Goddard's attendance at rehearsals. With her beady black eyes upon me, her customary supercilious smile playing about her lips, as if constantly expecting disaster, I frequently found my mouth getting so dry that my tongue seemed to fill my whole mouth and words came out either in an unnatural squeak, or failed to emerge at all. How on earth I ever managed the end of term plays at all, I don't know, but act I did.

Even when I did my level best to avoid getting chosen to appear in plays, somehow I still always managed to find myself roped in to play yet another starring role. Once, at an audition for some puppet play, peopled by the misshapen mistakes of our attempts in craft lessons to create puppets for the occasion, I deliberately tried to make a mess of the speech assigned to me, (something about a person who 'couldn't tell a badger from a polecat', as I remember). The speech itself was enough to floor me; after all, I couldn't tell a badger from a polecat, either, but I garbled my lines in an excrutiatingly inept manner, only to find, to my infinite disgust, that I was, in spite of all, chosen to play the unenviable part of the Princess, a puppet of remarkable ugliness, with asymmetric features and a gaudy gold lamé dress. Next I was forced to be in the obligatory Nativity play, playing the angel of the Annunciation, clad in a long white nightie and inadequate cardboard wings. Every time I attempted to take my role seriously and practise my lines at home, declaiming in ringing tones to the imagined Mary, "Hail!" Reggie always spoilt the effect by crowing in mocking tones, "Wind and rain!" which left very little room for optimism about the actual performance. Actually, long white nighties seemed to haunt me in plays. We never wore nighties or pyjamas at home: we went to bed in our underwear, so when, once again, I was chosen for the starring role in another play, about a little girl whose toys came alive at night, with my friend Edna cast as one of my dolls and a cheeky little boy called Mickey Terry as my golliwog, black face, striped trousers, fuzzy hair and all, I had to go through the mortification of borrowing a nightdress for the occasion from another child. Still, it must have all been something of a success, for people called me Jane (my name in the play) for months afterwards.

Morning assembly in the junior school was a sight to behold. Grey-suited Miss Goddard, sausage curls all immaculate, presided over the proceedings from the raised stage at the end of the hall. She decreed that we should sing the Lord's Prayer, not recite it, to a complicated tune that was just too difficult for us. We stood in rows, brows knit in furious concentration, swaying in unison from side to side, in a vain attempt at keeping the rhythm of the piece, piping in our broad Brummy twang. As this performance went on, Miss Goddard would become more and more enraged at our incompetence and the assault we were making upon her ears, and would frequently break into our recital with:

"How now, brown cow,
Grazing in the green green grass",

or

"A funny old man in blue, he blew and he blew and he blew.
He blew a balloon
As big as the moon.
That funny old man in blue."

in a totally mis-timed and ineffectual attempt to improve our diction and accent, and we would dutifully intone the rhymes after her, still in our broad Brummy accents, and then carry on with our incompetent singing, with scarcely a hiatus. Miss Goddard, forced to accept defeat with as much grace as she could muster, would then carry on with the assembly as if nothing had happened. She would teach us the words of hymns parrot-fashion, enunciating the words in an exaggerated way so that we should not get the words wrong; only we did get them wrong, of course. For many years I was most embarrassed to sing "The Lord is my shepherd I shall not want", thinking it rude and most ungrateful. What a difference a little punctuation makes!

The fiasco of the singing mercifully concluded, Miss Goddard invariably invited us in her posh accent to bring "flahs" for the hall and then swept out, her minions in her wake, leaving us to file out of the hall in an orderly fashion and go to our classrooms.

Academically, the juniors was much like the infants had been. We copied out poems in our best writing books, and gained coloured stars for good work. We did much arithmetic, wrestling with problems, and having few interesting books to read. The one really memorable time for me was when one of our teachers read us "The Wind in the Willows" and another teacher, who was a gifted artist, decorated the plain cream walls of the corridors with glorious full-colour illustrations of scenes from the book. Before my delighted gaze Ratty, Mole and Mr. Toad came to life. Mole fell in the river, Ratty taught him the delights of messing about in boats, and Mr. Toad took up motoring. To me the pictures were an enchantment, and I used to offer to run messages for teachers so that I could look at the pictures as I went about the school. It was one bright spot in the misery of the war, of school, of life in general. Yet, before I left the school in 1950, the Council, with that total lack of sensitivity and a callous indifference that so often characterises official bodies, had sent in the decorators, who obliterated with the regular cream distemper every one of the evocative pictures that had been the only thing that had made life bearable for me.

I spent three years in the junior school, yet I never really settled into it at all. The very lessons that might have been thought of as offering relief from the academic curriculum – art and needlework – were sheer purgatory for me. The teacher of these subjects, the hated Miss Brookes, was obviously oblivious to the tradition of kindly schoolmasters such as Mr Chips. Miss Brookes was straight out of the tradition of Mr Squeers. She was a tall, thin, angular woman, built like Popeye's girlfriend, Olive. Her nose was beaklike, her lips thin and mean and she seemed to have an implacable hatred for all children, particularly me. Nothing I did pleased her. In needlework, my chain stitch was deemed ill-formed, and had to be cut out, my running stitch was uneven and had to be unpicked, and with all the cutting-out and reworking she had decreed, my finished piece of work resembled nothing better than a grubby pin-cushion. In art, things were no better. My pictures were frequently screwed up in disgust and thrown into the waste paper basket, and such was my terror of the woman that even my drawing of a Christmas tree took on the ludicrous shape of a bunch of asymmetrical bananas. If it hadn't been for a boy called Paul Ducros, who was good at art and frequently helped me with my drawings (bless him!) life would have been even more unbearable than it was. As it was, I frequently told my mother on art or needlework days that I had an ear-ache, which was always guaranteed to get me a day off school.

Another form of torture dreamed up for our delight, and at which I wasn't much better than at art, was country dancing. Once a year we were decked out in head-dresses of artificial flowers and suitably rustic dresses; the boys were transformed into Morris dancers by the addition of ribbons and bells, and odd straw hats, and accompanying staves of wood, with which they enthusiastically assaulted each other, ensuring bruised knuckles and cracked skulls all round, and our proud parents were invited to the school to see us perform traditional country dances, which we danced to tunes such as "The girl I left behind me" and "Over the hills and far away". I, spineless and jelly-like as usual, wasted much nervous energy worrying about whether my mother would remember that I absolutely had to have the required headdress. Frequently, she arrived, breathless, just before the show was due to begin, with some adequately acceptable concoction for me to wear, but not before I had gone through agonies of embarrassment and shame.

In my second class, Miss Meredith's class, came the high-spot of my junior school career, as far as I was concerned. There was to be a grand school concert at the Town Hall in Birmingham, at which all the primary schools in the city were to perform. Our class was chosen to provide a group of singers to represent the school and, to my joy, I was chosen as one of these. I adored the daily trips by bus into town to rehearse with the massed choirs in the Town Hall: I was missing school, my bus fare into town was being paid, and I was appearing at the Town Hall, singing! All too soon, however, the concert was over, and the torture of school once more beckoned.

My only other contact with music in junior school was the time when Miss Goddard decreed that we should have a recorder group, to play at assemblies and concerts, and I eagerly joined. It became one of my most cherished ambitions to own a recorder of my own, and many a time when I passed Schott's music shop on the Coventry Road I stood, nose pressed up against the window, like Hungry Horace coveting a delicious cake all alone in the window, and out of his reach. I'd eye the dark brown descant recorders, long, smooth and sensuous to the touch, but far too expensive for me. The school owned a few recorders which were lent out to children who did not have their own instrument. These had a large distinctive piece of sticking plaster round them, bearing a number, so a check could be kept on which child had which instrument. As I stood in the rows of the assembled group while we played I was miserably aware of the sticking plaster, so messy and so very visible, that proclaimed to the watching audience that I was too poor to own my own instrument. I saw it as a sort of mark of Cain, and my being chosen to introduce the various items we played did nothing to lessen my feelings of shame.

Actually, this was the least of the mortifications that the recorder group bought me. My having started school so late meant that I had very few friends in school: their already established groups didn't need a latecomer – so when one of the girls in the recorder group suggested I go to her house after school so that we could practise together, I was overjoyed. I suppose every mother at some time has told her child that she disapproves of the company he keeps. Well, it was I who suddenly found myself cast in the unenviable role of unsuitable companion for my new friend. She lived in a road opposite the shops, in an unremarkable semi on the corner of a road of what my mother called 'the bought houses', and, so it appeared, this gave her mother pretensions to middle-class respectability, which, for some reason, excluded me. The girl was as colourless and unremarkable as I was myself, but I was considered not good enough to be her friend. When we went to her house straight from school, everything was all right, because her mother would still be at work, but if I called when her mother was at home (she was not, of course, ever allowed to enter the polluting confines of my home), I was treated to a disdainful look and left rudely on the doorstep while the girl was fetched to speak to me there. I couldn't understand what I'd done wrong, but that I wasn't welcome was made abundantly clear, not only by the mother but also by my friend's younger brother. He was a shrill-voiced, whining child, with the bloodless complexion of the middle-class prig, and fine, anaemic straight blond hair, scraped back and plastered to his little round head. The merest hint of a slight or injury rendered him hysterical: I thought him a first-rate cissy and couldn't help giggling whenever I saw him. Once, in one of his shrill rages he referred to some other boy as a "swine", a word that for some reason I found perfectly shocking. Had he called him a "sod" or a "bugger", I'd have let it pass as a familiar term of abuse, but a "swine" – that was language I was not used to, and I forthwith ceased to go round to their house, feeling that they were hardly the right class of companions for me.

With the end of the war came another innovation – men teachers. Back from the war came the beloved Mr Penny to take his top class once again. I fervently hoped to be in his class, for I was much frightened by Mr Dempsey, who took the other top class. My joy on being put in Mr Penny's class, however, was very short-lived, for soon afterwards he left the school and we were turned over to the decidedly untender mercies of Mr

Pearmain. We were used, of course, to raps over the knuckles with a ruler: that we could get from the women teachers, but Mr Pearmain was something else entirely. He set us arithmetic problems that we simply couldn't do, and kept us in every break and lunchtime to make us do them correctly. He had the terrifying habit of breaking into our silent work with sudden frighteningly loud shouts, which froze my brain and reduced me to abject terror. He became something of a bogey man to me, and even years later I was unable to cope adequately with arithmetic: a problem still brings me out in a cold sweat.

In the lunch hour, Mr Pearmain's frequent detentions notwithstanding, we were left alone to play in the playground. We were used to being left to our own devices and we pursued our games, each sex to its own games. The boys played football, of course, and their usual wild chasing games, while the girls played games peculiar to their sex. One of these which I, with my easily bruised sensibilities, found particularly trying and embarrassing consisted of a circle of girls, all holding hands and rotating round a single girl in the middle of the circle, singing the words:

"The wind, the wind, the wind blows high,
The leaves come scattering across the sky.
She is lovely, she is sweet,
She is the girl from the northern street."

It all sounds rather sweet and poetic now, but this pleasant rhyme was followed by a hurried conference between the ring of girls, who chose the name of some particularly obnoxious boy. The ring then re-assembled around the girl victim and the following verse was chanted:

" . . . (boy's name) says he loves you
All the boys are fighting for you.
Let the boys say what they like.
(boy's name) loves you so and always will . . . and that is true."

It all sounds so silly, childish and innocuous now, but then the shrill crescendo of the final words still come back to haunt me, and I'm back again in the centre of this hostile ring, putting my hands over my ears to keep out the noise.

One game which we all played with much enjoyment was "Film Stars". We were all mad about the cinema, of course, and we read avidly all the gossip about the stars in the movie fan magazines. Even the names had glamour to us and we invented a game where we could speak the names of our heroes. One child thought of the name of a film star, giving as a clue just the initials. As soon as someone guessed the name correctly, the person whose choice it was ran off, until someone else had the presence of mind to shout "Stop!" Then, the person who had guessed correctly had to try to reach the initial chooser in a prearranged number of steps, which, if she succeeded, gave her the right to choose the next initials. The sheer pointlessness of the game could hardly explain its popularity. Its appeal, of course, lay in the chance it gave us to speak the names of the celluloid heroes and heroines, and let a bit of their glamour rub off on us as we incanted their names. It was our only, tenuous link with the glamour epitomised by Hollywood and its stars, and it brightened our dreary, austerity-dominated lives.

I liked the sedate Film Star game, and hated the rough and tumble of the more boisterous games, of which Polly on the Mopstick was one. It was a game where physical injury was more than likely. Two teams were assembled: the biggest and strongest in the team stood back to the wall of the school, supporting a whole line of other team members, bent double, hanging onto the child in front, like a procession of circus elephants. The aim of the game was for each member of the opposing team to leap astride the backs of the bending team, sitting astride them long enough to cry "Polly on the Mopstick, one, two, three", before the row of children beneath them collapsed. If the line collapsed that team had lost, so the leaping onto the backs was both heavy and deliberately clumsy, in an attempt to make the line collapse. For the weak or unwary this was a game that inevitably produced scraped knees and ricked backs.

I preferred to join the little children in a gentle game of "Queenie", a ball game, where one person tossed the ball back over his head and one of the other children hid it behind their back, while the thrower wasn't looking. Then he had to guess who was holding the ball. Refinements such as making people turn round, or show one of their hands were introduced to add variety to the game, and many a small child let slip the ball from his grasp while trying to turn completely round without revealing his hands.

In our final year, of course, came the decision of whether or not to enter for the examination for the Grammar School. My mother was against my taking the exam, arguing that if I passed she could not afford the uniform that would be required. Gran promised that if I was successful, she would buy the uniform, so one foggy morning found myself and two other girls from my class who were sitting for the same school, on the bus across the city to Small Heath, off to the school where the exam was to be held. I had chosen this particular school because one of the two girls who accompanied me lived opposite a girl who was already a pupil at the school, which seemed to me to be a good enough reason for me to go there, too.

We walked nervously up Waverley Road, looking for the school and, after a false alarm, when we went into the church by mistake, we soon were in the school, taking the exam, watched over by the formidable Mr Mills. All I remember about the exam was 100 intelligence questions which I was proud to have finished in the time allowed, and the small cramped desk in the corner of a gloomy classroom where I sat to do my tests.

Exam over, we made our way home again, walking through Small Heath Park, glad it was all over. And that was that. No preparation, no anxious parents to take us to the school and to worry about the effects of such an ordeal on our psychological health, no feeling that our whole future depended upon the tests we had just taken. We merely went home, went back to school and were mildly surprised a few months later to receive the official brown envelope that told us whether or not we had passed. When the letter came to say that I had been successful and from the following September I would be a pupil at Waverley Grammar School, I was an object of interest to my parents and the other children for all of five minutes, and then we all forgot about it until the time came. In the strange way that these things have of happening, neither of the two girls I had been with to take the exam had passed, and so, come September, I went off to my new school alone. I was ten years old.

CHAPTER 5

After the War

Once the initial euphoria had worn off, the end of the war brought us nothing but problems. I don't know whether the common purpose the war effort had engendered in people had papered over the cracks of personal animosities and family conflicts, or whether the enormous strain, both

Me, after the war, aged 7

mental and physical, that the war had placed upon everyone suddenly began to take its toll, or quite what it was that caused it, but the return of the men from the war and the return to something approaching normal life seemed to bring out the worst in people.

Firstly, there was my uncle's return, to find his home being shared by four other people, not to mention his return to a wife and child to whom he was virtually a stranger. It meant nothing to him that it had been thanks to my parents' contribution to his household expenses that he had a home to come to after the war: he wanted his house to himself, to get to know his wife and son again after the long separation. The situation was further exacerbated by the birth, in 1946, of my sister. She came into the world during the night, late in May. Reggie and I, awakened by the noise of various comings and goings up and down the stairs, had come out onto the landing to see what was going on. A plethora of female relations were coming and going, bringing the traditional supply of hot water and other required articles. Aunt Liz, hushing our questions, ushered us swiftly back to bed, with the vague promise that we'd know all about it on the morrow. We didn't seem to be overwhelmingly curious, however, for we never heard the first cries of the new-born child – we were fast asleep. The first we knew of our sister's entrance into the world was the next morning when our father came into our bedroom to announce the happy news. We were quite disappointingly uninterested in the revelation until my father confided that the premature birth had left them unprepared, so that the new child was at present sleeping in my doll's pram. I must confess to a most unbecoming and unreasonable resentment on hearing this news. "Get her out of there!" was my first reaction, and I ran off downstairs to evict this interloper from my property.

I have reason to feel ashamed of my outburst, for I hated dolls and prams, and, in spite of my Gran's continuing to buy them for me, seeing them as suitable toys for a girl, I never played with them. Actually, I preferred to play adventure games with the huge teddy that Grandad had once luckily won at the fair. Reggie and I used to tie poor, long-suffering Teddy to the line post, pretending we were savages who had captured an intruder on our desert island. We sat on the sofa, pretending it was a ship, storm-tossed while bound for exotic foreign lands, and many a time Teddy fell overboard and had to be rescued by Reggie from the foaming, tempestuous sea. But dolls – definitely not!

Actually, my refusal to conform to what was expected of me caused many a problem within the family. Once, when I was about 7, I was given some money by a relative for my birthday and was taken in great excitement to a shop to buy some toy with it. As we went into the shop the first thing that caught my eye was a large, bright red fire engine, sturdy and wooden and with a bell on that really rang. I was fascinated by it and insisted on having it. Back home I took it in triumph, to run it over the rugs, over the tiles in the kitchen, where its wheels made a satisfying sound, out into the garden and down the path. I was so absorbed in my new toy that I failed to see the disapproving glances of my female relations: a family conference was hastily summoned, and the news was finally brought to me by my mother that it had been decided that a fire engine was an entirely unsuitable toy for a girl to have, and therefore, it was to be given up to my cousin, Buster, for whom it was totally appropriate, and I was to be taken back to the shop to buy something more suitable for a girl. In spite of my rage and my tears, my fire engine was taken away, and I was taken back to the toyshop where I was coerced into accepting in exchange a doll's tea-service and a mini baking set, as reflecting the legitimate interests of a girl. My mother carried them home: I wouldn't even touch them, and I never even took them out of their wrappers.

Soon enough, however, a pram was bought for my sister and my doll's pram was returned to me, to moulder unused in the bedroom, and we began to address the problem of the overcrowding in the house. We were now eight people in a small three bedroomed semi and my uncle and aunt who, it must be said, had always been selfish and malicious people, began to behave in a most disagreeable way to both my parents and to us children, in an attempt to force us to leave the shelter of their roof. For us it was a most worrying time. Reggie, who by this time was about 12 , felt the pressure very strongly and took the whole burden of worry on his own shoulders. The trouble was that in truth there was precious little that any of us could do. The extent of the bombing, coupled with the sudden homecoming of thousands of servicemen had created a housing crisis of epic proportions. Everybody's house was greatly overcrowded, with bombed-out relatives, returning menfolk, homeless children and displaced relations, and accommodation just could not be had at any price.

We listened on the grapevine for any hint of available accommodation, haring off to any address that came into our hands from any source, only to find, of course, when we got there, that it was already vastly overcrowded and we couldn't be squeezed in. In desperation we took ourselves off to a newly deserted army camp near the Yew Tree, rows of semi-circular huts, like air-raid shelters, made of corrugated iron, enclosed by a wire perimeter fence, in the hope that one of these huts might be available. To my intense relief, by the time we got there, every hut had been claimed by squatters, and all were fully occupied. My parents were almost tearful with disappointment: this was their last desperate hope, but secretly I was glad. I reasoned, quite rightly, that if we'd settled in one of the huts, unsatisfactory as it was as accommodation, the Authorities would just have washed their hands of us and turned to people who were truly homeless. I preferred to put up with the daily rows with Aunt Doll, the unpleasant atmosphere and the need for total silence about the house, so as not to give them anything about which they might complain.

We had another reason for not wanting to stay where we were. My aunt, when her son Buster had been born, (actually he was called Alan, but had been Christened Buster by another uncle when he was gorging himself at the street celebrations at the end of the war); had been wanting a girl. She had romantic visions of dressing the child up like a doll, and having a fairy-tale daughter, made of sugar and spice and everything nice, so, when not the longed-for girl appeared, but a snaps and snails boy, she had just rejected him. She treated him with a callousness that shocked us. Even the prisoners of war that I had been taken to see, interned behind barbed wire in Sutton Park, until they could be repatriated back to Italy, had just looked cold and dispirited. Actually, I'd been most disappointed in them. From the stories I'd heard of the enemy I'd expected them to, at very least, be horned and cloven hoofed. On seeing the dirty, dispirited, homesick men, my disgusted comment had been: "But they're only men!" They weren't ill-treated: Buster was. His mother couldn't bear him to wake up during the evening when she was listening to the radio or had gone a few doors away to drink tea with her mother, and the poor child was often beaten for interrupting his mother's leisure time. Reggie and I got into the habit of taking him into our bed if he woke up in the late evening, where we would amuse him and tell him stories until he fell asleep. His mother, when she returned and went to bed, never even noticed he was missing from his cot.

As time went on, of course, he saw us as his brother and sister and my mother as his mother, and so, his first reaction when he saw my new sister lying next to my mother in bed was, to push the new baby away, climb in bed with my mother and say, ominously, "We don't want her, do we, Aunty?" And he clearly didn't want her. As my sister grew up he became cruel and spiteful to her. We couldn't take our eyes off him when he was with her, or he would be hitting her or tormenting her in some other way.

Things went from bad to worse. My mother, scandalised by my aunt's treatment of her own son, and my uncle's quite unnaturally harsh disciplining of Buster, not to mention Buster's treatment of my sister, became more and more anxious to get away. We, Reggie and I, were very unhappy, and increasingly anxious as time went on. The tension in the house was hard to bear, and our aunt and uncle began to take on the stature in our eyes of horrible bogey-men. All this was further compounded by an incident that scandalised not only us but the whole neighbourhood.

One morning, Reggie and I were lying in bed, waiting for Mom to call us to get up for school, when we heard a great commotion downstairs, coming from Aunt Doll's living room. We thought we heard the word 'Fire', so we both leapt up and rushed downstairs, fearful that the house was burning down. We ran into the room to find my mother scooping up Buster from the floor, and enveloping him in a blanket, hastily snatched from her own bed. Aunt Doll sat in her chair, motionless, while Buster screamed like a banshee. He had, it appeared, fallen backwards into the open coal fire, burning both his back and his elbow, which he had thrust into the fire as he fell. We were abandoned to get ourselves ready for school, as Mom placed Buster into the pram and fled, taking him to the doctor to be treated. All through the chaos and confusion, Aunt Doll just sat in her chair, unable, or unwilling, to act. It would be charitable to put her inertia down to shock at the horrible accident that had just befallen her son, and, perhaps, that's what it was. But we, all too frequent witnesses of her callous indifference to her child, preferred, maliciously, to see her inaction as yet another sign of her maternal cruelty. Soon, of course, the whole neighbourhood knew of the incident, and for some time there were pursed lips and the accusing statement: "D'you know, she wouldn't even take him to the doctor's."

Unjust? Yes, of course, it had been just a shocking accident, but we felt a sort of twisted satisfaction in her being seen more widely for the woman she was.

This incident, and the more acute rancour and ill-feeling it had engendered, made it even more imperative for us to find other accommodation. We applied for a council house, hoping that, with the new housing boom that had followed the war, swallowing up bombed sites and empty fields, even fields of corn, a new house could be found for us. We received numerous visits from council officials, checking the details of our domestic arrangements. We embellished tales (albeit true in essence) of the curse of bed-bugs, that ate us alive while we slept, and much capital was made out of the impropriety of brother and sister, now fast approaching puberty, having to sleep in the same room. Actually, I loved the arrangement. Reggie and I were very close, bonds cemented through all the dark days of the war and mutual adversity, and he used to tell me the most exciting adventure stories at night before we went to sleep. We read comics together under the blankets, when we were supposed to be asleep, and we enjoyed our forced intimacy no end. But when the council lady came, of course, we sighed theatrically and told her how we longed to have a room of our own.

Every morning, after the visits from the various council officials, Reggie took to waiting anxiously for the postman, looking for the longed-for official brown envelope. After many fruitless vigils, finally his patience was rewarded one morning, when the postman held out a letter to him, with the words: "This is what you're waiting for, I think," and we waited in an agony of suspense while Mom opened it, to reveal that we had, at last, been allocated a council house, just a few minutes' walk from our present home, on a new estate, just created out of farm-land, on the other side of the school. A home of our own! It was beyond belief. We'd never had a home of our own: we'd always lived with relatives, first with Gran, then with Aunt Doll.

The news spread quickly. My parents began to treat Aunt Doll and Uncle Reg with something of the same malevolence that we had had to endure for so long from them. It was no longer necessary to placate them, to pander to their most unreasonable whims, to bite our tongues when an angry retort rose to our lips, and the last few weeks before we moved were a strange mixture of unbearable tension and exhilaration. Once the prospect of our imminent departure became a reality, hostilities ceased, and Uncle Reg, on our November 5th celebrations, offered us the most helpful advice. We were just about to light a banger in the back garden, mostly, I suppose, to frighten the little children, when Uncle Reg helpfully suggested that if we really wanted to make a big bang we ought to place the metal dustbin lid over the banger, which would be bound to make a monstrous explosion. We took his advice, he lit the touch paper for us, and we waited while the fuse spluttered into life. A deafening explosion rent the air, and Aunty's dustbin lid took off like a flying saucer, crashing neatly through the french windows, to land, blackened and somewhat crumpled, on the rug before the fire in the back parlour. We saw it as evidence of the existence of poetic justice and laughed about the incident for ages. Even Mom and Dad, when they pointed out the real dangers of our thoughtless behaviour, couldn't quite keep a smirk off their faces.

The last few weeks before the move were spent in collecting up our miserable store of belongings and ferrying them by hand, on a borrowed hand-cart and in our trusty pram, up the gully at the back of Aunt Doll's house, up another little gully, past the school and into the brand new housing estate, on the other side of the school, which was to be my home until I married and moved away.

Our final removal wasn't anything like the glorious affair I'd imagined. After all, I had argued to myself, such a world-shattering event as our ensconcement in our very first home of our own ought to be accompanied by tearful farewells from contrite relations, and a grand exit in some kind of mechanical conveyance. But it wasn't to be, of course, and, when the time came, we simply trudged off up the gully, clutching our last-minute bundles of possessions: and as we made our way up the gully, the frantic screams of the abandoned Buster followed us and tore out our hearts. "Take me with you, Aunty. Wait for me. I want to come."

All the way to our new house we heard the echoes of his heart-broken screams. I have never felt in my life since more desolate and guilty than I felt then. We were abandoning him to God knows what, and we felt like murderers. Even when we arrived at the new house we heard, or was it just our imagination, him crying to us and we were almost tempted to turn tail and go back for him. He was just like our brother and it was just like handing a lamb over to the wolf. In later years, this heart-tearing memory, and that of the suffering of that small boy was to come back to haunt us, for poor Buster was to die at the tragically early age of 39, from lung cancer.

Birmingham Town Hall 1950's

CHAPTER 6

Westcott Road

Our rather inauspicious move from the Grove to Westcott Road, creeping up the gully, bundles of possessions under our arms, rather like doing a moonlight flit, was not made any more edifying by Mom's finding two dead rats on the doorstep of our new house, and flatly refusing to cross the threshold until the offending beasts had been removed and placed in the

Westcott Road

57

dustbin, out of her horrified sight. She didn't even like white mice, so I suppose rats were hardly likely to make a favourable impression, even dead rats. Still, once this impediment to entry had been removed, we were able to take stock of our new home.

Unlike the Grove, Westcott Road was straight and flat. It was a long, narrow road, with asphalt and paved pavements and a road surface made of pre-cast concrete, laid in sections, with a broad, dark line where each section joined the next; (very useful as goal-lines in our games of football). Half-way down the road, neatly dividing it into two, was a round island. At first it was just an island with a mound of earth filling almost all its circumference, but after a time it was levelled and concreted over, providing a good bend for us to race our bicycles round. The two halves of the road, so arbitrarily divided by the island, always remained two distinct roads, and we had very little to do with the people in the other half. Reggie went to school with a couple of boys from the other end of the road, but most of the houses down that end were inhabited by people whom we only knew by sight.

The houses themselves were a strange mixture of the old and the new. Outwardly, they were old-fashioned; not even semi-detached, as in the Grove, but a long series of terraces, each of ten red-brick houses, each with a neat front garden. Access to the backs was via old-fashioned shared entries, rather like the old slums they had been built to replace. The entries were dark, narrow passages, with two gates at the far end, one for each house either side. The gates gave access to the kitchen door and the back gardens, divided from each other by a short wall and chain-link fencing.

Inside, the houses were both modern and old-fashioned in concept. The focal point, as in old houses, was the kitchen. It was large room, with a fireplace, behind which lay the back boiler, so that to heat the water you had to keep a fire in the kitchen. There was a large, heavy, crock sink and a weighty wooden draining board, just like in the Grove, but there was a range of built-in cupboards, and even a built-in dresser, with cupboards and drawers, all of which over the years built up an accumulated population of junk, so that to open a cupboard would bring a shower of useless and long-lost objects raining down upon your head. There was a recess under the stairs, to hang coats and store yet more junk that couldn't be crammed into the cupboards, and, near to the back door was the pantry door, so that if both doors were unwisely opened at the same time a sickening collision would occur. After one such accident the pantry door parted company from its hinges and was promptly chopped up into pieces to help keep the kitchen fire going.

Outside the back door, a mere couple of steps away, lay the outside toilet, next door to the coalhouse. At first, we still got wet fetching in our coal, but in later years the council erected glass roofs from the house to the coalhouse, making a sort of open verandah, so that going to the lavatory or fetching in a bucketful of coal could be done in relative comfort. The kitchen floor was tiled with smart red tiles that in future years would require a great deal of work on my part with the red 'Cardinal Floor Polish', to keep them looking decent.

From the kitchen led an L shaped parlour, with windows to both front and back. Mom was quite dismayed by this arrangement: she wanted a front parlour she could keep for 'best', so she nagged Dad into erecting a rather flimsy partition between the front part of the room and the back, leaving a tiny dining room, just big enough to house a table and four chairs, and a large front room, which she could leave as a best parlour. Actually, it didn't much matter, really, for we lived in the kitchen anyway, and the coal fire in the front room was very rarely lit.

Upstairs, there were three bedrooms and a tiny bathroom, with all the necessary equipment fitted in with the precision of a jig-saw puzzle. There was no heating in the bathroom and it was always icy cold. The main bedroom at the front of the house was large, and had a gasfire and a built-in wardrobe. The back bedroom had a small electric fire and a built-in wardrobe. The third bedroom was no more than a boxroom really, just big enough for a single bed and a slender occupant.

Many of the people moving into these new houses were, like ourselves, coming into space such as they had never known before, and we certainly found it difficult to acquire enough furniture to fill up all the space. The days of hire-purchase had yet to come. In a few years' time the dining-room suites in bird's eye maple and the uncut moquette three piece suites would make their appearance in every home, along with the china cabinets and fireside chairs, but for now we had to beg furniture from wherever we could. Gran gave us a couple of dining-room chairs and from somewhere Mom managed to scrounge three sideboards, all of different shapes, sizes and woods, but which were all somehow accommodated in the front parlour, where they soon became receptacles for all manner of unwanted clutter. Mom also managed to become the proud owner of an enormous chest of drawers, with a thick wooden top as large as a mortuary slab. She said she'd only accepted the offer of it because the wood was too good to waste, but, of course, no-one ever quite got round to using the wood for any other purpose, and in the meantime it had to be found a home. Finally, we were all pressed into reluctant service to manoeuvre the doughty giant up the stairs and into the large front bedroom. Getting it round the bend at the top of the stairs and onto the landing was sheer purgatory. My sister was crushed between the massy form and the banisters, where she screamed while we tried desperately to find a crevice in which to ease the chest so as to allow her to breathe, and Reggie and I crouched beneath the huge weight on the stairs, rather like Atlas, to support it with our backs so that it wouldn't just slip straight down the stairs again and wreck the hall. Finally, however, it rested in the bedroom and, as we ruefully surveyed our various injuries; scraped knuckles, ricked backs and bruised shins, we swore that we'd never move it again. Nor did we: it just stayed there for years, gathering dust and junk.

Decorating the house also proved to be a bit of a problem to us. It was painted with regulation cream distemper, which my mother said, "got on her nerves", so we were set the task of finding a cheap way to decorate it. Some families, of course, those with older children at work, could afford wallpaper, but all we had was ingenuity. My father's contribution to the effort was confined to a large tin of peach distemper and two small tins, one of green and one red which he had gained from someone at work. His part of the task finished, he promptly repaired to the pub and left us to get on with it. Unfortunately, all we owned were two paintbrushes, one for Mom and one for Reggie. Loth to let me escape the work, Mom prowled round the house in search of something that might serve. Finally, her hopeful gaze fell upon the brass companion set on the tiled hearth of the front parlour. Triumphantly she picked the round sweeping brush from the little brass stand and declared that I could use that. With an air of foreboding, my protests that a round brush wouldn't do at all stifled by Mom, who declared that I must do my bit, I took the brush, dipped it into the peach distemper and applied it to the wall, promptly spraying myself peach from head to foot. My shrieks were dismissed by Mom as over-reaction and she grudgingly provided me with an old scarf with which to cover my hair, and I was instructed to carry on painting.

However, Mom decreed that plain peach walls were 'too plain' and we had to find a way of jazzing them up a bit. We took balls of string, scrunched them up in our hands, dipped them in the red and green paint and applied them to the peach walls, rather like primitive abstract stencils. From the window, we agreed, the irregular red and green pattern might just be mistaken for wallpaper. A neighbour, who always had a taste for excess, came round with a tiny tin of gold paint, which she proceeded to shoot in a fine spray over the walls, to give it all, as she said, 'the final touch'. So, for many years, we lived with this tribute to the invention bred of necessity, until the day when Dad managed to come by some Chinese wallpaper . . .

Having got used, after a fashion, to having so much space, we then had to get used to having many neighbours. In the Grove there had been only 12 houses, most of them occupied by relations, but here we were all strangers, brought together by a shared need for a roof over our heads. We soon learnt who was friend and who was foe. Our chief friends were the Butler family, who lived over the road at the end house. When we first knew them they had four children, two girls and two boys, but after my last sister was born in 1950, Jessie decided she wanted another child and gave birth to Roger. Jessie Butler was a Yorkshire lass, warm, generous, loving: a sensual woman of great physical appetites and love to spare for all – rather like an Elsie Tanner character. Her husband, Albert, was a meek, tall, angular man, slow of speech and thought, a man of great good will and quiet kindness, but no match at all for his firebrand of a wife, whom he could not satisfy either socially or sexually. I used to listen to the women gossiping when they didn't know I could hear, and from them I learnt that tha Butlers' sex life was far from satisfactory. I worked out later that poor Albert had suffered from premature ejaculation and his wife's consequent sexual frustration led to their life being a series of violent explosions of emotion. At least, they were violent on Jessie's part: Albert remained in the face of all provocation quietly-spoken and mild of manner, which totally infuriated Jessie. She once, in a rage, hurled a full tea-pot at him. Fortunately, he had had the presence of mind to duck at the right moment, allowing the teapot to strike the kitchen wall with a force that smashed the pot, sending tealeaves and boiling water all over the room. What drove Jessie into paroxysms of rage was Albert's typical reaction to the eruption of this violence: he merely quietly picked up the pieces of the shattered pot, and took a cloth to clean up the water.

She had, it appeared, only married Albert because he had asked her, and, at nineteen, and fearing she was already on the shelf, she had thought it prudent to agree. They were totally incompatible in every way; she a flamboyant, larger-than-life personality, he, totally lacking in imagination. He'd even registered their second son as 'Albert', after himself, because he didn't have the imagination to think up another name on the way to the Registry Office! Such a union, of course, was bound to fail, and, ultimately, it did, but not until Albert had tried the experiment of working away from home, in Scotland, while Jessie, tired of looking after five children on her own, had hatched the plan of dispatching the children alone on a bus to Scotland for Albert to take care of, telephoning him at work to warn him of their arrival. Reconciliation brought nothing but tragedy, for Jessie became pregnant again and in a desperate attempt to end the pregnancy, almost killed herself. My mother went over to her house one night to borrow some household article, to find Jessie in the process of bleeding quietly to death on the floor of the kitchen. Mom's prompt intervention, calling an ambulance straight away, saved Jessie's life, but caused a great deal of scandal and alarm in the neighbourhood. Every child in the area, I suppose, sometimes, when sent to search in a drawer in Mom's bedroom for some lost article, came across a box of mysterious pills, which Mom wouldn't explain about. Whether any of them did induce abortion I doubt; after all, Jessie had had to resort to a knitting needle. This scandal was later to be followed by that of Jessie running away with the husband of a lady round the corner, leaving Albert to cope in his slow, quiet way with raising the children.

Chief amongst our foes as children was the hated Mr. Batchelor, who lived three doors down from us. He would never allow us to retrieve any ball that went into his garden. The garden consisted only of flattened down earth, with a few scrubby-looking conifers dotted about it at rare intervals (he was no gardener), but to ask him to return a ball that had dared enter his domain sent him into great rages. He was surly enough to the adults: to the children he was an ogre, as evil-tempered as his wife was kind. Once, Tony, who lived opposite us, dared to offer him a mouthful of cheek just as he was in full spate, and to everyone's absolute astonishment, Mr Batchelor came charging out of his garden, where he had been pawing the ground like some enraged bull, and launched himself out of the front gate and after the startled Tony. Caught off his guard by the sudden attack, Tony was slow in starting running, but with Mr. Batchelor in hot pursuit, red in the face both from rage and from the unaccustomed exercise, he streaked off down the road in search of some sanctuary. We groaned as we saw him turn into what seemed to be a dead-end – the entrance to the school, guarded by a six-foot fence. With an energy born of sheer desperation, Tony vaulted clean over the fence, scrambling clear into the school playground, just as his pursuer's hand clutched at his disappearing heels. Unnerved by this experience, we gave Mr. Batchelor a wide berth after that, but we all took great malicious pleasure in retailing to anyone who would listen, the juicy gossip of Jessie Butler's assertion that she had met him on a train with a woman who was not his wife, and he had been most embarrassed at the encounter.

The neighbours on our immediate left were most interesting to me. The mother was a widow, with one son and three daughters, all grown up. What interested me was the glamorous fact that all three girls were 'on the stage', though I never really discovered what any of them actually did. They were remarkably tolerant neighbours; the girls never once complained when our puppy stole their stockings off their washing line, ruining them in the process. In a period when she was 'resting' from her stage work, one of the girls decided to open a dance school, in a room in a local school. I was in heaven. I was invited to join and learn ballet, tap and acrobatic dancing. I was so excited when I went to my first lesson, though I don't suppose I learnt very much at it. Then, I discovered that the lessons cost 9d a week; the lady had omitted to tell me that. She insisted that as a friend and neighbour I could have lessons free, but my pride wouldn't allow me to accept charity that she could, no doubt, ill afford, and, as my parents wouldn't entertain the idea of parting with 9d a week for mere dancing lessons, I never went again to the class. Even then, as now, 9d seemed a small price to pay for an escape from the harshness of everyday life.

To the right of us lived a family who seemed rather alien to us; too good for a council house. Many of the residents, such as the Wilsons a few doors down had been rehoused from the inner-city slums, but the Cooks were far more genteel. The father was a kind, quiet, remote man, who was soon to die of tuberculosis, a mere stickman, whom my father had to help lay out in the middle of one night, though there was seemingly only a skeleton to lay out. His wife, a fat woman, given to adolescent giggles, rejoiced in the rather pretentious (to us at least), name of Phoebe, and we generally ignored her, except to ridicule her refined accent and call her 'the honourable Feeb' (which was how we pronounced it). Their children, Anne and Teddy, were weak, gently-nurtured creatures, totally unused to the rough ways of a council estate and we had great pleasure, Reggie and I, in splashing them unmercifully at the swimming baths, and deliberately picking flowers from their garden to reduce them to impotent rage.

Others of the neighbourhood were better off than we were, if not in the same class as the Cooks, because they had older children working and bringing money into the house, but we also had our share of the 'problem families' that I'd first encountered in the Grove. The Stones, who lived over the way, in one of the 'tin houses', (so called because they were faced with corrugated steel cladding), showed all the classic symptoms of deprivation. The husband was a work-shy, drunken brute; the wife, a sluttish woman who worked as a barmaid at night, leaving the children to roam the streets to all hours of the night, to the scandal of the neighbourhood. The eldest daughter, no more than a child herself, was left to keep the family together and keep the smaller children cared for as best she could.

Just over the road from them lived a family, just as poor and even more numerous, yet totally different. The Milligans were a poor Catholic family from Glasgow, presumably removed to Birmingham to find work. They were fiercely Scottish: Mr. Milligan would have nothing but the broadest Scottish burr spoken in his house. His own accent was a thick slab you could carve with a knife, and all the children were totally bilingual. In the house they resembled caricatures of the archetypal Glaswegian, but in the street and at school they were undistinguished Brummies, just like the rest of us. Their brood of children grew steadily year by year, and it seemed that soon they would be like the old lady who lived in a shoe, of nursery-rhyme fame. That they never became so was thanks to their habit of packing each of the sons of the family off to join a Scottish army regiment, just as soon as he was old enough to join up, thus leaving room for the next addition to the family. We loved to see the boys when they came home on leave, in their tartan kilts and plumed hats. Charlie, who had an affinity with animals, and particularly with birds, once delighted us by having as a pet a jackdaw, whom he taught to speak, and once he even raised an orphaned eagle chick.

The only other family with whom we had much to do lived four doors away from us. They were the Winns, and we played with their children. The father was a long-distance lorry driver and my father sometimes used to go on his long trips at weekends, to keep Bill company and to get out and about a bit. I remember them most for a most beloved bull-terrier pup they once gave us. Bill had a friend who bred Staffordshires and as he had already given Bill the formidable Bruce, a massive bruiser of a dog, built like a table, flat topped and with a leg at each corner, when his friend gave him a bitch, his wife refused to countenance two dogs and so we became the grateful owners of Bessie, who gave us enormous love and devotion, not to mention numerous litters of cross-bred puppies, and bruised legs from her thick tail which beat like a metronome as she lay under the dining-room table at mealtimes, waiting hopefully for scraps. Mr. Winn wasn't as popular with my mother as he was with us, however, for he once called at our house one weekend drunk, and behaved rather aggressively, and from that day she was reluctant to have him in the house.

All in all, with the exception of Mr. Batchelor, of course, we were quite a compact little society in our end of the street. As for the people who lived in the other half, however, on the other side of the island, they might have been on a desert island for all we saw of them. We saw the parents coming up from work of an evening and we occasionally knocked on a door in search of change for the gas meter, but that was all. Sometimes, when Mom was making toffee to make us toffee apples, the children from the other end would be drawn down to our end, led by the nose, by the delicious smell of treacle toffee that wafted up the road. But, their toffee apples duly provided by Mom, who wouldn't see any child go without, they generally just made their way back to their own half of the road to consume their sticky, dark-brown apples, held rather precariously on scrubbed lollipop sticks, saved especially for the occasion. This apart, our lives met but rarely.

CHAPTER 7

Daily Life

Truth to tell, the brave new world we had fondly imagined we would find in the new house just didn't materialise. Post-war life was tougher than ever. We had accepted rationing and the sheer misery of shortages during war-time, but once the menace of Hitler had receded and we no longer had to put on a brave and united face to combat him, we had expected things to get better, but all that happened was that the misery went on. Not only was food still rationed, and consequently hard to come by, but money began to be a real problem, and frequently I was despatched on a humiliating errand to take rationed goods (our rations, of course), to a better off family in Duncroft Road, at the bottom of the Grove, to sell them, to raise cash for some other more pressing necessity.

True, there was no more need to fetch coal: it was plentiful for those who could afford it; and afford it we had to, for the coal fire in the kitchen could not be allowed to go out. Our whole comfort and livelihood depended upon it. The heat from the fire heated the water in the back boiler, for washing and washing up, for an immersion heater, which ate up shillings like a child devouring chocolate buttons, just couldn't be afforded. Indeed, we very rarely could afford shillings for the gas or electricity meters, which seemed to have a voracious appetite for them, and many a time the fire in the kitchen was all that stood between us and disaster. The fire, flickering and uncertain, was sometimes our only light, and frequently our only means of boiling a kettleful of water, or of toasting bread, which we held out on a spindly iron toasting fork into the flames and smoke.

We soon learnt how to make our meagre resources of coal go a long way. The coal dust, the 'slack', was shovelled into buckets and mixed with flour and water into a modgy paste. Then we pulled out great sticky black handfuls, shaped them carefully into round bricks, which we left outside to harden. We would light the fire with a few pieces of good coal, and once it was well alight, the large, home-made cannonballs would be placed on the back of the fire, topped off by cabbage stalks and potato peelings. Round the fire would be placed the huge brass fireguard, not in case the children should burn themselves, but simply as a frame to hang the wet washing to dry, on rainy days. The fire itself remained invisible to us, but we heard it spluttering and hissing like an angry dragon as the water in the peelings dried out, sending out clouds of smoke that gave both the kitchen and the washing a grey tinge and a smoky fragrance.

Finding enough food for us to eat was, so it seemed to me, even more of a problem than it had been during war-time. Perhaps because as I grew older it fell more and more upon me to take responsibility for feeding the family, I was acutely aware of what it meant to be too poor to buy the necessities of life. Some days, when we hadn't been able to raise enough money to buy anything for our dinner, Mrs Butler, who may have been luckier, would make an enormous stew, containing anything edible she could lay her hands on, and her five children and our four would share the steaming saucepanful of vegetables and gravy, mopping up with bread to help fill the empty corners of the stomach. The arrangement, of course, was reciprocal: when we had food, they dined at our table.

Actually, food would have been even more of a problem had it not been for that blessing of the poor – local credit. All our local shops were small family businesses, except for the George Mason grocery chain shop. Gaining credit from chain stores wasn't possible, but local shops had to offer their customers credit, or there wouldn't have been any customers during the week. Mr. Gee, our local fish and chip shop owner, sensing a good business opportunity, changed his chip shop into a small general grocery store, just a few doors away from George Mason's. His gamble paid off, if not exactly handsomely, at least well enough for him to make a living, for he offered what we couldn't get anywhere else – weekly credit. Goods "on the slate" all the week: settle the bill on Friday when you get paid. We had to pay Mr. Gee's bill, of course, if we paid no other, else he wouldn't give us credit the following week, and we just wouldn't eat. I would take notes to Mr. Gee from my mother, he would provide the requested grocery and put the amount on our bill, which Mom would settle on Friday. The only hiccup to this system came if Mr. Gee was in a bad mood, or a child was pert, or if he thought someone was asking for too much; we were, after all, at the mercy of his whims, but, generally, we ate from Monday to Friday courtesy of Mr Gee and his little general store.

The worst, most humiliating, way of raising money to see us through the week, in my eyes, lay in the pawn shop. On Monday mornings, when I was at the Grammar School, I used to have to take a bulky bag, containing my father's best (and only) suit, so that after school I could take it to the pawn shop, where I could obtain for it the £2.10s, without which we couldn't have lived through the rest of the week. I hated the job, not least because of the evasive answers I would have to give my schoolfriends when they asked where I was going after school, and what was in the big bag. I don't suppose anyone actually enjoyed going to the pawn shop: for me it was a bitter humiliation. The shop was in a row of mean little, old-fashioned shops in Green Lane. The front of the shop was just that: an uninteresting window full of what looked like junk. To get to the 'pledge department' necessitated going down a sordid, narrow, dark entry and through a large door, painted in a dark colour and badly scuffed by the many hands of the poor upon it. The room itself was poky, dusty and gloomy, with piles of labelled bundles stacked high all round, on shelves behind the plain wooden counter, worn smooth by years of pitiful transactions conducted across its surface. These bundles were the 'pledges' left by the clients in exchange for small sums of money, in some cases very small sums of money, for in those days money would be lent on virtually anything. Poor old ladies would offer bundles containing little more than a couple of threadbare blankets, which meant they would be even more cold in bed at night, and would be lent a couple of precious shillings on it. Pretty well no-one was turned away: even a shilling was useful. These worthless old things could never have been sold, of course, 'to defray expenses', but the pawnbroker knew full well that he'd never have to sell them: the pledges would all be redeemed at the end of the week. They had to be or you'd not be able to come back again on Monday and raise a couple of shillings again. My father's suit, a made-to-measure affair in lovat green, made at a discounted price by the father of a mate, was worth £2.10s as a pledge, for it could, if necessary, have been sold; to us the money was priceless, for it would help us struggle through till Friday, and pay-day. I should have to return on Friday after school to reclaim the suit, so that my father could wear it at the weekend when he went out drinking with his mates, but it could be returned once more on Monday, to spend the working week in the pawnshop, alongside the other bundles.

I absolutely hated the journey to the pawnshop, to the run-down row of shops where it was. I imagined that everyone on the bus knew where I was going and was sneering at me for my poverty. I sat on the bus in my school uniform, the offending bag containing the suit on my lap, self-conscious and convinced that my guilty secret was common knowledge. Pathetic though it was, the only consolation that I could offer myself for my humiliating errand was this: just near to the pawnshop, in the same row of shops, right near the bus-stop where I got the bus home, was a most run-down and miserable-looking barber's shop, with a window containing very little else but the dust of ages and a few faded photos, curled at the edges and brown with damp and age, of hair-styles and of famous faces advertising hair-products, hair-cream, shampoo and the like. In a dusty, gloomy corner of the window, only visible if you really looked for it, was an ancient photo of the film star, Alan Ladd, advertising what, I don't remember. I was at that time very much in love with Alan Ladd, my first real fantasy idol, and I consoled myself for my horrible experience of the pawnshop with the promise of this tantalising glimpse of my idol before I caught the bus home. Of such miserable, laughable, petty consolations is a young girl's comfort made!

Buying clothes, even after the war when they were no longer rationed, was another problem to be surmounted. In the early days, before the advent of mail-order and credit, the way that poor people managed was by means of the 'club cheque', a scheme often run at factories. The workers all paid a few shillings into the club each week, and each week it became the turn of one of the members to receive the 'Provident Cheque', which they could exchange at one of the participating shops, for clothes and other necessary items. It was just a simple way, of course, for poor people to save for what they needed, without using a bank (I never knew anyone who had a bank account), but it was also a way of exploiting the poor, for only a limited number of shops participated in the scheme and so you had to accept goods from a very restricted number of shops, which limited your choice enormously. My Gran, who had promised a school uniform if I passed the Grammar School exam, bought my uniform on her 'Provident Cheque', and, since Grammar School uniforms were only available from one exclusive store in the centre of Birmingham, I spent all my school career dressed in traditional pleated gymslips instead of the four-gore pinafore skirts which were our school uniform. Nevertheless, it was a real red letter day when Gran's cheque became due and we could go off to a shop and choose new winter coats or new shoes. To my shame, I remember assuring Gran that the glamorous red shoes that I was trying on were absolutely perfect for me, for I was so determined to have them, when in fact they were at least a couple of sizes too small, and having to suffer for my untruthfulness by having shoes that pinched most uncomfortably!

In the 1950s a new way of buying clothes came in which had a short but exciting vogue – that of the clothing company reps who called on householders once a week, providing goods, which could be paid for by means of weekly payments. £20 worth of goods could be had for a weekly payment of 5/-. My mother, dazzled by the prospect of having new clothes instantly available at such little cost, fell into the trap of so many people in her position, and ran up debts that she just couldn't hope to pay off. Friday nights thus became a nightmare for us, as we played the game of hiding from the rep, in search of his money. We skulked in every possible hiding place, to try to keep out of sight when we heard his knock on the door. Partly, I suppose, because the reps were responsible for the debts they had allowed their customers to run up, they were tiresomely intrepid in tracking down those reluctant to pay, and were not above coming round the back if you failed to answer their knocks on the front door, to peer through the kitchen window in an attempt to winkle out their recalcitrant customers. After a while, of course, it occurred to the companies that our estate was a bad financial risk, and the reps stopped calling, but it had been good while it lasted: we'd had new clothes whenever we needed them. Then we slipped back, after this little interlude, to hand-me-downs and make do again. I remember being utterly amazed once on hearing a lady in our street tell a neighbour that she'd just washed her son's new trousers, unworn, so that the material would be soft to his sensitive skin. What wouldn't I have given for the feel of brand new material next to my skin!

The Friday night game of hiding from the clothing company rep, lurking in the pantry or under the stairs until we heard the sound of his car receding into the distance, was a thing of the past, but the pantomime of hiding from the rentman was an ongoing sport that lasted for years. Dad never knew, or cared, about our money worries. He simply handed over the housekeeping money on Friday and believed that his duty was done. He then repaired to the pub, leaving us with the perennial headache of just who to pay before the money was quite used up. It was always a question of robbing Peter to pay Paul, and sometimes the debts mounted, while my father remained quite oblivious to the worries that hung around us all the week.

When it was the rentman's turn not to get paid, we went through all the same farcical charades we had used to employ to avoid the clothing club reps, only with the rentman it was rather easier. After all, it wasn't his money, he was merely a collector, and it was not his concern if we fell into arrears and had to be evicted, so he never bothered to try to ferret us out if we failed to answer his initial knock on the door. We still huddled in our hiding places, though, just in case, hardly daring to breathe lest he should suspect our presence, and once, when my little sister, who had been carefully briefed to keep silent when the man came, shouted cheerfully on hearing his knock at the door: "We're not in!" our hearts nearly stopped, but if he'd heard her he gave no sign, and he just went next door to see if they were paying that week.

I once called upon Mrs Butler to borrow something for my mother. Having knocked at the back door, I went straight in, as was the custom, only to find Jessie and the two girls crammed into the tiny space under the sink, their usual hiding place from the rent man. He was called, rather menacingly, 'the agent', as if he were as lethal as a latter-day spy, and so, I suppose, to us he was. The day he called was always nerve-wracking for me: it must have been pretty horrid for them, too, for there was a great turn-over of staff and the 'agent' was rarely the same man for long; although whether this was because their singular lack of success in collecting the rents in our street got them sent packing, or whether they just gave up the job, unable to stand the suspicion and hatred of the inhabitants, I don't know.

During one particularly tough time, financially, Mrs Butler hit upon a rather novel way of paying the rent. She sub-let one of her bedrooms to an itinerant Irish couple. It was strictly against the terms of the tenancy, of course, and heaven knows how Jessie, Albert and five children managed to share a three bedroomed house with two other people, but Mr and Mrs Connolly certainly helped to pay the rent for a few months, until their wandering spirit took them off on their travels again. The husband, "my Barty", as his wife proudly called him, was a shadowy figure to us children, for he worked long hours and was consequently rarely encountered, but his wife was often to be glimpsed, popping into the neighbours' houses for a cup of tea and a cadged cigarette, and her thin figure, as angular as a clothes horse, clad in lumpy, brown, well-worn boots, with curled up turnovers, (which she wore in every season), was a familiar sight, going from door to door in search of a cup of tea and a gossip.

CHAPTER 8

The Children's Lives

Parents and children in Westcott Road, led entirely separate lives, for the most part. Some mothers stayed at home, of course, to look after the little children, but most parents worked and the street life of the children didn't impinge upon the adult world at all, except for those rare times when their children fell foul of the law, or injured themselves and had to be taken to hospital. David Wilson, trying to show us how clever he was by climbing out of the bathroom window onto the glass roof of the verandah, crossing the roof and then jumping spectacularly from the coalhouse roof into the back garden, tried his party piece once too often and fell through the glass roof onto the paving stones below, which necessitated fetching his mother from work to take him to hospital to be put together again. I was frequently breaking bones during the course of our boisterous games, the results of crashing falls onto the hard concrete road, usually, and so had regularly to be taken to the Accident Hospital for yet another plaster to be applied to the wounded limb.

When Tony, who fancied himself as Westcott Road's answer to Al Capone, believing himself to be, like Byron, 'mad, bad and dangerous to know', set up a nice little line in bicycle stealing, using the local youngsters as thieves, while he got rid of the ill-gotten gains, purloined from the unwary, parents were, of course, inevitably drawn in, for the little children, frightened of what they had got themselves into, spilled the beans, and the whole unsavoury business came to light, earning Tony a short stretch in Borstal.

People went about for a time mouthing in tragic stage-whispers that he had been 'sent away' , but he soon returned, and not too long afterwards we had the hilarious sight of our local tough, richly greased D.A. haircut shorn to near baldness, doing his stint in the army, neat, tidy, disciplined, and finally a pillar of the establishment. He had, in truth, never been nearly as tough as the image he liked to project. True, he and I had once got into a most unseemly tussle over some minor incident, rolling about in the dusty gutter, punching, scratching and kicking, spitting and hissing like a couple of tomcats, but a boy who can be upset that Bing Crosby should be made to record the song 'Hello, young lovers' soon after the death of his wife, and could be terrified out of his wits by finding under his bed one night a Guy Fawkes, made for November 5th and forgotten, can't qualify as being exactly in the same league as a Ronnie Kray!

Tony's bicycle stealing, of course, never included the taking of any from our estate: it just wasn't done to steal from your own. In any case, nobody owned a bicycle worth stealing in our road. The currency for locomotion for us was generally the feet. We walked everywhere: outings, cinema, parks. Only when we had to travel into the city centre, or across town, to the roller rink, at Walford Road, did we use buses. Mechanical conveyances of any sort were a very rare sight in our road. The most popular of these, as far as us children were concerned, was the soap-box trolley, made from four old pram wheels and a stout plank of wood, joined by a nut and bolt at the front to a cross-piece, which held the front wheels and allowed the trolley to be steered. Any child who owned one of these was wooed and cosseted, in the hope that he would allow you to ride on it, and many a feud arose between the favoured few and the rejected majority.

One day, from where I don't remember, we came by an old coach-built pram with four large spoked wheels and a sturdy chassis. Gleefully we dissected the body, reserving the wheels and the back of the pram to be attached to our finished trolley as a comfortable back-rest. One of the neighbours gave us an old plank, rather battered, but thick enough to suit our purposes, but whose thickness raised problems of how to drill a hole right through to take the nut and bolt. Reggie found a drill amongst the junk in one of the cupboards in the kitchen and to our immense pride we managed to construct a most superior conveyance, which even boasted a brake: only a piece of wood attached by a rather dangerous-looking nail to the rear of the plank and which was pushed in a most primitive way onto the back nearside wheel, it was true, but it was a brake all the same. The other children, as we wheeled it out into the street for its maiden test-drive, were all suitably awe-struck. And so they might be: IT WENT LIKE A DREAM. Time and again we sped down the hill of Billingsley Road to the bottom, dragged our heavy trolley back up and sped down again. The exhilaration of the triumph was only spoilt for me by my catching my dress on the nail of the brake and tearing a gaping hole in the skirt, but, Mom apart, everyone was delighted with our new machine, and couldn't wait to try it.

Reggie, by this time having tested his brainchild sufficiently to satisfy his ego, went home, leaving me to make the magnanimous gesture of offering a ride to all the little children. They crowded on, no-one wanting to be left out, so that not an inch of the trolley was visible. Gleefully, we pushed off to make our exciting descent of the hill. It was only as we gathered speed and the bottom of the hill loomed ever closer that I realised to my horror that the sheer weight of all the passengers, pressing down on the front of the trolley, meant that the force on the front nut and bolt, holding the front axle, was so great as to prevent my steering the machine at all. I hung onto the steering ropes, tugging with all my might, but to no effect. As we hurtled down the hill, approaching with a terrifying speed the kerbstone at the bottom, I realised that this was, in a very real sense, the crunch. When it came, it was most spectacular in its effect. We hit the kerb with enough force to send all the little children flying in all directions, scraping knees, cutting elbows and tearing knees out of trousers all round.

Complaints were made to my mother by aggrieved parents. I was treated like some mass murderer, as if something after the massacre of the innocents had taken place, and Mom, who was the law in all matters of discipline in our house, forbade the use of the trolley again. I tried tears, wheedling, bitter complaint, but to no avail. It was no use appealing to my father: discipline wasn't his province, it was Mom's, so my beautiful trolley remained impounded in the back yard, until the weather and disuse had done its work and it was reduced to a heap of rusting scrap metal.

Several of the children owned bicycles of sorts, most of them of ancient vintage and uncertain parentage, and which boasted no refinements such as brakes. They were stopped, in an emergency, by the time-honoured practice of sticking the left foot in the spokes of the front wheel, with all its attendant risks of shredding the shoe and amputating the toes on the wicked spinning spokes. Many of the bicycles were made up from bits of old ones salvaged from tips or resurrected from junk heaps in back yards. We called them A.S.P.s, (All Spare Parts), and we had great fun with them, having races up the road, round the island in the middle and back home, or having bicycle speedway races on the grassy field down the road. When we lived in the Grove, Gran had once bought Reggie and me brand new bikes, to replace our much despised babyish tricycles, and had been reduced to frozen horror as we rode them at full speed down the hill of the Grove, straight over the main road at the bottom of the hill and then clean down the gully that led to the back gardens of the houses in Duncroft Road. How we were never killed, she, and we, never knew.

One year, my mother, given to rash promises, promised me a new bicycle for Christmas. I allowed my imagination to run riot, dreaming of a bright red machine, resplendent with much gleaming chrome, to outshine the dull, mongrel concoctions I usually rode. I painted graphic pictures to the local children of just what this fabulous machine would be like. Christmas came, and to my disappointment and horror, the finances, of course, hadn't been able to run to anything more than just another A.S.P., painted a dull, matt, uniform black all over. Even the wheel rims, which should have been gleaming chrome, were painted the same dreary, dull black, to cover up the rust. Ungrateful I may have been, but I was deeply ashamed of this blow to all my hopes and I was most reluctant to ride it and face the jeers of the other children, who, perhaps, knew all along that I was bound to be disappointed.

For most of us, our houses were merely places where we slept. The back gardens were for growing vegetables, or for leaving as a wild place for the local cats to meet and stalk birds in; the front gardens were just for show, with a bit of a lawn and a large privet hedge screening it from the pavement, useful for pushing enemies into when some violent altercation took place, but we lived and played in the street. There were very few cars (indeed, for many years, no-one in our street owned a car), so there was no fear of our being run over, and our society was totally street-orientated.

The currency of the street was the ball. Anyone who owned a ball of any sort, tennis, foot or rubber, was sure of a high place in the hierarchy of the street society, for our lives revolved about ball games. All the young children were coached by their elders into becoming expert throwers and catchers and kickers of a ball, or they could not have taken their place in the exclusive society of the street. Without such skills, a child was an outcast. We took a ball with us everywhere we went. If we went to the cinema we took a ball to play with on the long walk there and back, and even when I went to the Grammar School I still played football all along the street to the bus-stop.

We had an inexhaustible number of ball games to play. The line in the concrete road served as a goal line and we played football in the street under the light of the street-lamp until late into the evening. This same streetlamp served in summer as a place to chalk wickets on, the other wicket being chalked on the pig-bin on the corner of the road. Well into the 1950s the pig-bin stood on street corners, receptacles for all left-over food scraps, to be collected by the council and boiled to make food for pigs, and our bin was just conveniently positioned to act as our second set of wickets. Jessie Butler's dad was a Yorkshireman, who knew the importance of cricket, and when he came for his yearly holiday with the Butlers, every summer, he carved us rough cricket bats from pieces of old wood, and the cricket season started the first day of Jessie's dad's holiday and finished when the last of the bats finally gave up the ghost. If a nosy policeman should come along while we were playing (ball games were forbidden in the streets), we could always drop the bat into the pig-bin and wander innocently and aimlessly about the street until he was safely out of the way. The balls we used were usually soft – no-one in our street ever owned a real cricket ball, until years later when Reggie found abandoned an old ball with no leather cover, and we used that. At least, using a soft ball generally saved us, and the windows, from damage, except on the occasion when Buster, practising a particularly elegant stroke while defending his wickets chalked on the back gate, put the bat clean through the dining-room window with his graceful follow-through.

Most of our ball games, however, required no more equipment than a ball of some sort. For "Cannon" we needed to purloin four clothes pegs to make a rough wicket shape up against the kerb stone in the road. This was bowled down by the captain of one team, which then set in motion a rapid chasing game, the ball being passed swiftly between the members of a team, all trying to strike members of the opposing team with the ball, to eliminate them from the game. When all the team have been eliminated, then the roles are reversed. It was just yet another version of the old favourite "Hot Rice", which was much the same, but which did not require the peg wickets, and "Stick", where the targets for the ball were stationary rather than moving.

The ball game that gave the most fun, as well as causing the most injuries, was roller hockey. Roller skating was a pastime much in vogue, and most children owned a pair of battered old skates with metal wheels, which we attached to our shoes by straps and clips, which ultimately tore the soles off our shoes, and for which a 'key' was required to tighten the clips. The metal wheels made a most grating metallic screeching on the pavement, and the game was every bit as rough as any professional game in the National Hockey League. We played in the roadway, using the kerbstones to bounce the ball off and therefore to keep it in play, and for sticks we used our mothers' brooms, borrowed when she was not looking. The lines across the concrete roadway were goal lines and two scratch teams fought out in this primitive arena the most ferocious games. No parts of the anatomy were safe from injury, for no quarter was given or asked for. Scraping the legs or arms along the sharp edge of the kerb was common, and to go sprawling onto the asphalt of the pavement risked gravel in the knees. The casualties amongst the brooms were equally high: my mother simply couldn't understand why her yard broom kept falling to bits – the head just didn't seem to stay on the stale at all. To be a goalminder in this sport, and only the toughest or the most naive would take on the job, was tantamount to inviting death, for you were likely to end up face downwards on the concrete, pressed uncomfortably against the kerbstone, with a heap of other players pressing you down, with skates, fists and brooms flying.

With a regularity it was impossible to explain, the seasons for the various games came and went. For a while every paving stone on the pavement would be full of chalked numbers, bearing children's initials, (their own 'beds') in numerous hop-scotch pitches, and pieces of slate and flat stones were carefully saved and jealously guarded to be used as counters in the game. For weeks all that could be seen was groups of children, the little ones puffed and wobbly as they balanced on one leg, the older ones poised and superior, throwing their slates accurately and claiming their own 'bed', where they could put both feet down and take a rest from hopping from number to number. My youngest sister loved playing the game with young David Wilson, for he was an easy-going lad who let her cheat shamelessly.

Then, as if by magic, the hop-scotch beds would disappear, washed away by the rain, and we all had pocketfuls of marbles to play with. Mom's sharpest knife would be used to gouge holes out of the tarmac of the pavement, and all down the road groups of serious-faced children played their games, totally absorbed, for marbles were at stake. You didn't play with your favourite marbles, because if your opponent struck your marble then yours was forfeit, so it didn't do to play with those you didn't want to lose. The rules were complex, and many arguments broke out about who was 'fudging' (moving his arm nearer to the target marble than allowed) or just whose turn it was. Once you had your marble in the hole in the pavement you had the right to aim at your opponent's marble and it was just as well to opt for 'feet'. This meant that your opponent had to place his feet in a 'V' shape behind his marble, so that if you missed his, the marbles would not go spinning into the road or into a garden. It must have been a funny sight, with lots of children standing along the pavement, feet pointing outwards, like so many large penguins, far from their home!

The gods of the marble season were ball bearings. You couldn't actually play with them, of course, because, being metal, they were heavy enough to shatter glass marbles on impact, but to possess one gave the owner great kudos. When Reggie became an engineering apprentice, he used to bring me ball bearings from work sometimes, which gave me much currency of superiority in the hierarchy of street culture. Even now, if I find a ball bearing in the street, I still snatch it up as a great prize, and the satisfying sound of the shiny silver balls clicking smoothly together, still brings back vivid memories of life and death struggles for possession of other children's marbles.

In fine weather we used to borrow a length of Mom's washing line to play skipping games. We stretched the rope across the road from one side to the other, with a child each end to keep the rope turning, and we moved in and out of the turning rope to many different rhymes of indifferent poetic quality.

"All in together, girls
Never mind the weather, girls,
When I say your birthday, please run out . . ."

had us all running out of the turning rope when our birth month was chanted. Anyone who tripped on the rope had to take a turn at turning it, so it paid to be nimble. Emptying and filling the rope in this way was a favourite game and many rhymes existed that required such movement in and out.

"As I was in the kitchen, doing a bit of knitting,

In came the bogey-man and I ran out."

being one of the least poetic!
The older girls used rhymes that required difficult movements to be performed while still continuing to skip:

"Jelly on the plate, jelly on the plate,
Wibble-wobble, wibble-wobble,
Jelly on the plate.
Sausage in the pan, sausage in the pan,
Turn around, turn around,
Sausage in the pan.
Baby on the floor, baby on the floor,
Pick him up, pick him up,
Baby on the floor."

which gives an insight not only into our skipping games but into our daily lives and diet!
Other rhymes came from comic characters:

"Korky the cat, Korky the cat,
Korky the C A T."

Indeed, comics played a great part in the culture of all of us. We all had 'The Dandy' and 'The Beano' when we were small, and begged Mom to make us Desperate Dan cow pies, complete with horns, hooves and tail poking through the pie crust! I loved Lord Snooty and his Pals: to me it was not in the least incongruous to see a boy in frock coat and striped trousers; I thought all upper-class people dressed like that! Hungry Horace always struck a sympathetic chord in us, for fancy cakes were just as much a dream for us as for Horace. When Horace saw his cake in the shop window; always just one cake, either a large Swiss roll or a fruit cake with icing, and always marked 5/- we couldn't help feeling a pang of longing for it, just as Horace did.
As we got older, Reggie and I bought the comics with stories in, 'The Wizard' and 'The Hotspur', whose main aim, so it seems to me now, was to give working-class children a vision of the possible. Not only were the

heroes invincible, they were working class. 'Limp-along Leslie', the footballer, had a fellow player, Ishmail, who was a gypsy, and Alf Tupper, working-class rough, beat all the nobs on the athletics track. Even 'Wilson', the ageless man, who excelled at every sport, mysterious and with no past, seemed to give us the idea that you didn't have to start as somebody to be somebody, which thought I found strangely comforting, for I'd never been of much importance to anyone in my life.

We also gained other heroes to worship, and from a most unexpected source. Mrs. Batchelor, wife of our implacable enemy, had relatives in America, and after the war they came for a visit, bringing food parcels, new clothes and other goodies for their poor English relations. Along with the food they brought a real treasure for us children – American comics. We were amazed by them: thick as books, in full colour and full of a whole series of new heroes. Our favourite was Superman. We often used the magic word, "Shazam!" to help us get out of sticky situations, and we took to tying the arms of our coats round our necks, letting the coat stream out behind us in a pathetic imitation of Superman's cloak; and those of us who wore glasses breathed a huge 'thank you' to Clark Kent!

The comics were passed lovingly from hand to hand, and even our parents liked them for their novelty value. They weren't so keen, however, on the horror comics, with their gruesome illustrations, which we found fascinating. We were, in a way, most privileged children to have in this way a pre-view, so to speak, of the society that was to come to dominate the world in the next forty years. I only wish I'd been able to keep some of the comics: they simply fell to pieces from use.

During the day, with both our parents at work, we used to find many inexpensive ways of passing the days. One of our favourite pastimes was fishing for tiddlers in a local pond. My father was a keen fisherman, often going for weekends with his mates to Bewdley to fish in the river, and bringing us home baskets of cherries in the season, but our fishing exploits were very much low-key affairs. A garden cane, a loop of wire pushed into the end of the cane, threaded with a piece of old stocking with a knot in the end, was our fishing equipment, along with a jam-jar to bring home our trophies in. Clad in our wellies, in case wading into the pond became necessary for any reason, clutching a bottle of water and pieces of bread and margarine to keep hunger at bay, we walked to the nearest pond. It was on some waste land, quite a way from where we lived, a tiring journey for my little sisters. Once there, however, all weariness was forgotten, for there were little creeks to explore and undergrowth to play in if fishing for newts, sticklebacks and tiddlers palled as a pastime. We started fishing as soon as we got there, dredging up nets full of slime, water-snails and a myriad of tiny creatures to be sifted through and dropped into our jars. Newts were much admired as trophies and even sticklebacks conferred status on their captors, but, sadly, we never managed to get any of these wonderful prizes home alive, for they all seemed to expire on the journey back, so that all Mom saw was a jar of murky water in which floated abominable looking objects, rather like pickled specimens in a biology laboratory. I read somewhere in a comic that to keep the fish alive you needed not a jam-jar, with a wide top, but a pop bottle with a screw top, but all this change of receptacle did was to ensure that the fish arrived home boiled, and just as dead. When we tired of fishing we could wade about in the water, getting our wellies full of muddy pond water, which would guarantee a happy squelching all the way home as we walked.

We even at one time took to making the long trek from home across to Sheldon, to Birmingham Airport, which, in those days, was small and very exclusive. We used to spend all afternoon watching the aeroplanes and their privileged passengers flying off to exotic destinations. Outside the airport was a large finger post, fingers pointing in all directions and bearing such glamorous names as Paris, Berlin, Madrid, and Rome. When we tired of dreaming of foreign parts we could always make our way a little along the Coventry Road to Tiger's Island, a wild, open space, full of bushes, little brooks and hills, where we could have adventures, being cowboys and Indians or wild tribes, at least until tea-time.

In the Spring and Summer we would go off to Chelmsley Woods, which now is a sprawling council housing estate, ironically for the poor such as we once were, but which then was real woods. We spent all day playing hide and seek in the woods, paddling in the streams, keeping a weather eye out for leeches, which were rumoured to inhabit the water. We climbed trees, hid in hollow tree-trunks, and then picked the wild bluebells and the exotic blooms of the rhododendrons, pink, purple and bloodiest red, to take home to Mom. She wouldn't have the heady scented hawthorn blossom in the house, declaring it 'unlucky', and she rejected outright the brilliant rosebay willowherb as 'weeds', but she loved the rhododendrons and bluebells. After a long day's playing, however, we were usually so tired that the journey home always seemed that much longer than the outward journey and many a sad bunch of bluebells, crushed, their dark blue flowers withered and their stems limp, would be abandoned at the roadside by a child too tired to carry them any further, or end up a tragic patch of blue in the dustbin at journey's end.

Nevertheless, and though we wandered quite widely, always unaccompanied by any adult, we never came to any harm that was not of our own making. We got wet in the streams, our feet hurt from walking, we got stung by nettles and had to treat them with rubbing dockleaves on the affected spot, which left us with green streaks all down our legs like the war-paint of a primitive tribe, but we always managed to get home safely, even if I did usually have to carry one little sister piggy-back style the last few yards; and we grew up to be both independent and resourceful.

Our local cinema, The Tivoli, Yardley

CHAPTER 9

Family Life

From my earliest days I'd been something of an isolated child – firstly away in hospital, which cut me off from family and from other children who might have been my friends at school; and when we moved to Westcott Road nothing much changed. Of course, I took part in the street life, playing games, going to the cinema, standing in groups on the corner of the road, talking, gossiping, throwing a ball in a desultory way to each other, which useless pastime led the overbearing, disapproving old lady who had followed the Prices as our next door neighbour to prophesy in triumphant, crowing tones to my mother that "That girl'll come to no good, hanging about on street corners with boys!" but I still felt myself out on a limb, different from all the others and consequently increasingly unhappy. In a very obvious sense I was different from them, of course: I went to the Grammar School while all the others went to the local Secondary Modern, but my feeling of isolation went deeper than that. What weighed down upon me like a crushing weight on my whole life was the incredible awfulness of my family life, which made me feel both hopeless and stifled. Sometimes I used to feel that my whole life was like a pocket with a hole in it: dark, cheerless and empty – an uncaring void into which I dropped my most precious treasures – my hopes, my aspirations to a better life – only to have them slip through the hole and be lost.

I'd endured the hard life in the Grove, my long stays in hospital, the pain and isolation as any youngster endures life: as something inevitable. It washed over me and I just went along with the tide and accepted everything that happened to me without complaint, as being the natural lot of a small child, but as I grew up in Westcott Road, I felt an increasing need to take charge of my life, while at the same time being dragged along by a destructive undercurrent that threatened to submerge me at every turn. That destructive current was my family life.

As a child I'd had numerous instances of the insensitivity of the adults to my feelings, as the fire-engine incident had proved. Indeed, it never seemed to enter the head of adults that children had any feelings, or at least none that needed to be taken into consideration. All my relatives were under the delusion that they knew everything and could do everything, as I was to find out to my cost. One Christmas I had been given as a present a new watch, of which I was inordinately proud. I was still a very thin child, with a skinny little wrist which meant that, even on the last hole in the strap, it was still too big for my tiny wrist and slipped round my arm. When we were at Gran's at our traditional Christmas family gathering, I showed my assembled relations my new present, and my uncle commented, "Oh, look, the strap's too big. Give it here," he offered gleefully, "and I'll fix it for you." With the eyes of my family upon me I could do no more than hand it over, with palpable reluctance, to his untender mercies. For ages numerous relations wrestled with the problem, offering advice to each other, while I hovered anxiously in the background. Finally, after much head-scratching and mutual recriminations they were obliged to admit that the strap was ruined and would never fasten again. A quick search of the house unearthed a horrible piece of faded black ribbon upon which my lovely new watch was threaded and knotted about my wrist "until we can get you a new one after the holiday". I was heartbroken: my pride and joy was an ugly ruin, and I took myself off to lock myself in the bathroom and sob silently for my spoilt present, while, having dismissed the whole debacle from their minds, the adults got on with the party downstairs.

This total lack of sensitivity to the feelings of children was exactly echoed in my parents' treatment of their own children. They were not wilfully cruel to us: they were just so totally immersed in their own unhappiness that it never entered their heads to think that we might be unhappy too. It was a policy of benign neglect. Ironically enough, the very thing that brought all the simmering discontent to the surface was that wonderful, dizzy-making event that we had foolishly seen as being the saviour for us all – a house of our own. In a very real sense, Westcott Road was to be the catalyst that caused the irrevocable unravelling of the family.

During the war, with my father away fighting, or working in the Home Guard to defeat the menace of Hitler, there just hadn't been time for personal problems and antipathies to surface. Anyway, we'd all been too busy presenting a united front to Aunt Doll and Uncle Reg to waste precious energy fighting each other. When we moved to Westcott Road, however, all that changed. For the first time in their lives my parents found themselves thrown back on a close relationship such as they had never before experienced. They had spent all their previous married life living with relatives, first with Gran, then with Aunt Doll, in a sort of community living where the children belonged to all the houses and there was no such thing as a nuclear family. In any case, in time of war everybody's private life had been to some extent on hold. Now, however, in a home of their own, thrown back on an intimacy they had never known, they found fundamental differences bubbling up to the surface, differences that would finally destroy their marriage.

Mom was one of seven children. Her father had been gassed during the First World War, and had only survived for three years after the war. Her mother, devastated by the death of her husband, had, according to Mom, just gone into a decline and died finally of a broken heart. By this time, Mom was fifteen years old, having two younger brothers, still at school. Her eldest sister and her husband were promised a council house, on the understanding that they offered a home to the younger children, which, to their eternal credit, they did. It must, however, have been an awkward situation all round, especially for the older children, who realised what a strain they were putting upon the early married years of Rose and her husband. Early marriage must have seemed a convenient way out of a difficult situation.

My father's family lived just a few doors away from my mother's, in Kingstanding. My father had two brothers (one of whom was mentally retarded and lived in a home), and two sisters. The near neighbours met young and married early. It was not a marriage made in heaven: indeed, it was to prove to both, as well as to their four children, more like hell. They were entirely different in every way. My father was a young working-class lad, popular with the opposite sex, fond of drink and spending time with his mates, intelligent: (he had in fact passed the Grammar School exam but had not been able to take up his place because his parents couldn't afford to buy the necessary books). My mother was a young innocent, totally inexperienced about life: indeed, she only found out about the 'facts of life' when she gave birth to Reggie, a year after her marriage, at the age of 20. She was quiet, didn't drink, didn't enjoy pubs or a boisterous social life, and intellectually was nowhere near on a par with her husband.

They married, it appeared, because my mother was an attractive girl, and, flattered that my father, who had many girlfriends, should single her out for attention, used this flimsy reason as reason enough to get married. They never really got on together. My father was too young to want to settle down, and my mother couldn't understand his irresponsible attitude. The major bones of contention, right from the start, as is so often the case, centred on money and sex. In truth, money need never have been scarce, for my father was always a hard worker, always in work, and earned good wages as a skilled metal spinner. He never, I imagine, gave my mother enough housekeeping money, and he never saw as his responsibility the running of the household and its expenses. His duties ended with the handing over of the money on a Friday night. From then on, his time and his money were his own. In his defence I suppose it must be said that this was not an unusual attitude for working-class men of the time to take. To provide financially for the family was the limit of their duties. Being away at the war, when the whole responsibility fell upon the women, helped to reinforce this attitude. Evenings and weekends were free for him to pursue his interests with his male friends, leaving his wife to take care of the children and home, and as long as there was a meal on the table when he returned at night, and the children were not too much nuisance to him after a long day at work, then family life was running well. The man had his fishing, his drinking, his football; the woman had her home and children. Discipline in the home was my mother's sole responsibility. She enforced the rule of law, with the broomhandle if necessary. My father never once laid as much as a finger on us: it just wasn't his job.

On Friday evenings, when my father came home from work, I would be despatched to the draper's shop to buy him a new white collar (he always wore shirts with detached collars); he would don his only suit, (which I had just redeemed from the pawn shop) and, dinner eaten, he would go out to the pub with his mates, not returning until late at night. Actually, I'm not altogether sure whether or not he really knew where his best suit spent its weekdays. I strongly suspect it was just another of Mom's secret money-raising schemes that Dad knew nothing about. Saturday, if he was not away fishing, or riding with Bill Winn on a long journey, was usually spent in the same way. Lunchtime was spent in the pub: he would return home for lunch, sleep all afternoon, then, another meal eaten, would repair to the pub again for an evening session. My mother, not surprisingly, was very resentful of this pattern of behaviour: she hated being left in charge of the children all weekend, while he went out enjoying himself and wasting money that she could make better use of. It was, in fact, a moot point whether my mother could make good use of any money. Her ability to allow money to disappear without her having any idea where it had gone, was quite awesome. Money came in on Friday, and was totally gone by Monday morning, (hence the necessity for the trip to the pawn shop on Monday afternoon). Any money that was given to us children, by relatives, workmates, friends, who would slip my mother half a crown, 'for the children', never quite filtered its way down to us, but nestled for a brief moment in my mother's purse, before disappearing, along with all the rest. Indeed, it was never a good policy to leave money about the house: it had a tendency to disappear.

This rather unedifying pattern of life, scraping a way through the weekdays, with the help of Mr. Gee and the pawn shop, was transformed at the weekend into violence of nightmare proportions, when the other bone of contention between my parents, sex, came into play. After his many forays to the pub at weekends it was my father's habit to return home, late at night, expecting his conjugal rights to be readily available to him. My mother, full of resentment of his neglect of her, was more often than not moved to refuse his demands, and then all hell broke loose. I used to get out of the way at weekends as much as possible, but even I had to return at night and go to bed: and there I stayed, many a weekend, frozen with terror, hiding my head under the blankets so as to blot out the sound of the shrieks, of breaking ornaments and other, more unmentionable and sinister noises. I was too frightened even to cry out or to try to stop the violence: I merely used to wait, with my younger sisters, for the noise to die down, so that we could go back to sleep. I later learnt, of course, that the silence was often bought at the expense of my mother's giving in to the demand, for the sake of peace.

Sometimes, the violence erupted in the evening before my father went out, or at lunchtime before he went out to join his friends. One afternoon, the house seemed strangely tranquil for a Saturday lunchtime. My little sister, who was about two, was sitting on the rug, in front of the kitchen fire, playing, when my parents began yet another argument, I don't remember about quite what. My mother, to make a point, flounced off to the front door step to fetch in the bottle of milk that no-one had thought to bring in. As she came back into the kitchen, milk-bottle in hand, my father, who was standing in the doorway between the kitchen and the dining-room, went a bit too far (though I don't remember what he said), but Mom just went for him with the bottle of milk, cracking it neatly over his head. The noise, the shrieks of rage and pain from my father, the scream of triumph from my mother, allied to the terrified wailing of my sister, frightened by the sudden noise and the shower of glass, blood and milk that rained down on her from above, paralysed me for a moment, until I had the presence of mind to scoop up the howling, terrified child from the floor and take her to sanctuary upstairs.

Many times we were forced, after some such cataclysmic argument, to put on our coats, Mom, Reggie, me and the girls, and go out and walk the streets, passing the time away until it got dark, whereupon we could be fairly sure that my father would have gone out and it would be safe to return. Many a time we spent perhaps a week, living only upstairs, camped out in the big front bedroom with the gas fire, only venturing down during the day when my father was at work or out with his friends. Messages would be passed by us between our parents: "Mom says do you want any dinner cooking tomorrow?"

Then, after a time of such uncomfortable living arrangements, a truce would be called in the hostilities, and we would all resume what passed for normal life in our house, until the next time, that is.

After a while, my mother saw the chance of salvation. She thought she would get a job and thus ensure herself a measure of financial independence. She had, over the years, many jobs, usually in factories. First she worked for the fire manufacturer, Valor, which entailed her getting up at 5am, to get into work for 7.30. We liked it when she worked, first for Burton's Biscuits and then for Kunzle's cakes, for we always had samples of their wares on Fridays. Truth to tell, Mom's working didn't seem to have any appreciable effect upon the family's financial prosperity. Where her money went, I don't know, but we didn't seem to have any less financial headaches with her working than we had had without, and I was most distinctly worse off, for it was upon me that the burden of caring for the family, cooking, cleaning and shopping, now fell.

On school days I had to get up my younger sisters, see that the older one was ready for school, wash and dress the little one and take her over the road to Mrs. Butler, who minded her, and then, I just had time to abandon the house to chaos and go off to school myself, a journey of several miles. On my return from school I was expected to call at Mr. Gee's for the shopping, then clean up the house, doing the washing up and other tasks left over from the morning rush, and to get the dinner prepared and cooking for when Mom came home from work. She was frequently dissatisfied with my efforts, running her finger along the mantelpiece to ferret out dust and remarking sourly: "You haven't done this very well, have you?" and complaining about what food I had cooked and how much I had spent on it.

My mother often had to work on Saturday mornings as well, so I was expected to spend all morning minding the younger children, cleaning the house well from top to bottom, to make up for the skimping during the week, get in the shopping and put the dinner on to cook for when she came home. In the school holidays I looked after my two sisters as well as Mrs. Butler's five, leaving me with seven children to amuse throughout the long days. In between my domestic duties, of course, I had to fit my homework from school.

The only thing that made life even tolerable during this awful period of my life was that I had a sanctuary to which I could repair when the stress got too great to bear – my Gran's house. My Grandad, by reputation, was gruff and tough, and, so it was said, had not always been very kind to his wife, but to me he was kindness itself. It appeared that I very much resembled his dead mother, and I was always his favourite. Reggie and I had more or less been brought up by Gran and Grandad during the war, and we always had a close bond with my grandparents that the two younger girls never had. I was always given everything that Grandad could afford, and I basked in their affection, for neither of my parents took much interest in me. Indeed, I always seemed to be the odd one out. My mother doted on my brother, as her first-born and only son, and my father was quite close to my younger sisters, for not only had he been at home when my younger sister was born, but also by the time of their births he was old enough to have lost some of the wildness of youth. I, however, had spent most of my childhood away from home, and I never seemed to fit into the scheme of things, except as a maid of all work.

All this, however, was redeemed by the kindly affection of my grandparents. My Grandad, as far back as I could remember, had worked nights, as a machine minder in a factory, and when we lived in the Grove,

Reggie and I used to go round every morning to my grandparents' house, before we went to school, to share Grandad's breakfast of sausage meat. Many Friday nights I stayed with Gran, to keep her company overnight while Grandad was at work. This gave me all Friday night and all Saturday to enjoy being the centre of attention, and I revelled in it. On Friday evening I lay on the rug in front of the fire, cutting out pictures from newspapers and pasting them, with a paste made from flour and water, over the words in other newspapers, thus creating fat, lumpy, all-picture newspapers, which I took home on Saturday evening to show my Mom. On Saturday morning I went to the shops to fetch the dog biscuits for Gran's dog, Bobby, a brown and white spaniel cross, with long spaniel ears and a hang-dog expression. I'd play with the biscuits on the table when I got back; I was fascinated by their many colours and different shapes, oblong, round, diamond-shaped, square. I even tasted one of the black ones once, intrigued by the colour, only to find, of course, the unpalatable taste of charcoal!

Saturday lunchtime always meant stew: huge helpings of vegetables and meat, floating in a delicious sea of thick brown gravy. I always was reluctant to go back home after tea, and leave this haven of peace where I was secure and much loved.

As time went on, and life at home got worse, I used to go to my Gran's house every evening after finishing my homework. I always managed to arrive just as "The Archers" was beginning on the radio and Gran and I used to listen together. Reggie and I spent many summer evening playing cricket in Gran's back garden, stealing Grandad's raspberries off the canes at the bottom of the garden, and felling his prized gladioli with injudicious strikes of the ball. The younger girls never came with us: Gran's didn't mean the same to them as it meant to Reggie and me. Ironically, my younger sister was named after my Gran, yet Gran never liked her, and they rarely met.

I had even more of a reason to go to Gran's later on. One day, when a particularly violent altercation was in progress at home between my parents, Reggie, who by this time had grown into a burly teenager, had tried to intervene on my mother's behalf. A most unseemly tussle had then ensued, after which my father, in a towering rage, ordered him out of the house and told him never to darken the parental doorstep again. I'm quite sure that as soon as commonsense and sobriety returned, he bitterly regretted what he'd done, but by then it was too late, for Reggie had gone to Gran to tell her what her errant son had just done, and been offered shelter under her roof. He was to spend several years living peacefully with Gran, while I coped alone with the chaos of home. My only relief was to go to Gran's, to recharge my batteries in the peace and calm of a quiet household, and with the moral support of my brother.

Not that Gran's was always so peaceful. At Christmas the tradition was that all the children and the grand-children should congregate at Gran's house during the afternoon for a grand Christmas tea. There were usually us, Aunt Doll and her family, (by this time she had given birth at last to her longed-for daughter, born just a month after my youngest sister, in 1950, and predictably, just as spoilt and doted on as Buster had been neglected). Uncle Bill and his family came, and Aunt Maud, who had by this time married a small, meek, genteel man with very poor eyesight, attended the congregation with her husband and daughter, Janet. What a strange sight they made: Maud large, lumpy, angular, looking strong enough to fell a tree single-handed and the slight stooping figure of Arthur, feeble and genteel. Janet, it was rumoured, was a backward child, but it may well be, as my mother sniffily asserted, that anyone would be backward if they had to be brought up by such obviously incompetent parents as Maud and Arthur. Actually, poor Janet, we all agreed, had a great deal to put up with. Maud, it must be admitted, was intellectually lacking herself, and Arthur, brought up to leave everything to a doting mother, and afterwards to Maud, had no idea how to run a house and look after a child, and so they lived in a permanent state of quiet chaos. For some reason it never occurred to them to buy presents for their child at Christmas, so it was left to everyone else to provide her with toys and sweets, so that she would not feel left out of the festivities. The party was completed by Aunt Lizzie and her family, so we were a great multitude who spread over from the back parlour to the 'best' front parlour, noisy, boisterous and quarrelsome.

All through my teenage years this was to be the pattern of my life. My mother went out to work, made new friends, bought new clothes. My father worked all week, which he thought entitled him to spend the weekend drinking with his mates, while I struggled all week to keep the ship afloat as best I could, now without even Reggie to share the burden. If my mother thought to leave me 3d when she went out to work I'd lunch on a few chips while going through the grinding chores like an automaton, trapped in a joyless existence that seemed just to go on and on. I occasionally went out when I could borrow a decent pair of shoes from my mother, and my chief outings consisted of visits to the cinema, mostly with Reggie. We were children of the cinema age, Reggie and I, an age where you could go to the same picture palace three times a week and see three different programmes of films: one ran from Monday to Wednesday; another from Thursday to Saturday; and yet another film played on Sundays. Thus, we could see three different 'B' movies starring Gene Autry, the singing cowboy, in the same week, which, so Reggie opined, was enough to put you off the cinema for good! My only other outings were swimming with Reggie on Sunday mornings, and trips to the roller skating rink, where I could risk life and limb in style, wearing hired roller skates actually attached to the boots and with large, silky-smooth wooden wheels that whispered over the wooden rink in a most seductive way.

Looking back now, it seems to me that what made my life so unbearable to me wasn't just the sheer monotony, poverty and lack of hope that seemed to make up my daily round, but the feelings that this joyless existence engendered in me about my parents. When I was very small they'd been people who visited me in hospital and bought me nice things. Later, they'd been just 'my parents', a matter of some indifference, but as the burden of caring for the family and trying to keep our collective heads above water fell increasingly upon my frail shoulders, I began to be most judgmental about them, and viewed them with an exasperation that bordered on contempt. I reasoned that with the money they both earned (and my father had always been a hard worker) we should have been able to lead if not a life of affluence, then at least one which offered some shreds of respectability. It shouldn't have been that we regularly ran out of necessities such as tea, toilet paper or soap. We surely didn't need to have on our beds a few threadbare army surplus blankets, cut in two to make them double thickness, supplemented on very cold nights by my father's overcoat. (Actually, the only time the army blankets performed any kind of service was some time later when I used a convenient brown one to make a costume for my sister for a school play. With the addition of a few bits of wire and paper leaves I was able to transform her into a tree, looking suitably brown, green and wooden!) I began to rebel against the fate that decreed that we shouldn't even have an iron to press our clothes with, the

Aunt Maud (front left) with Mom, Reggie and Aunt Doll (back left)

last one having been dropped by my careless sister, and that when we sat in our two inches of tepid water in the bath, in a freezing cold bathroom, we had to sit at the taps end because the plug-hole was filled with a bit of rag that leaked, the plug having, like so many things in our house, mysteriously disappeared. (My only consolation in this hardship was that at least I had first-hand experience of the dreadful maths problems that I was so often forced to do, about filling baths that leaked!)

We didn't really have to find the spectre of debt behind every door and round every corner. My parents blithely took out hire purchase agreements on furniture, which they conveniently forgot to pay; the television spent so much time shuttling between our front room and the showroom that we hardly got to see any programmes, and I was constantly being sent to the shops on Friday (payday) to buy basic essentials that we'd had to do without for most of the week.

Without my taking my father's suit to the pawn shop on Mondays we would have been penniless all the week, and yet, even with the precious pawn shop money coming in I was still sent out begging at the neighbours' homes all week for a cigarette for my mother, who hadn't any money left to buy any. I crawled from house to house, trying to cadge the required cigarette from anyone my mother thought might oblige. If one refused I'd be sent out again with the words, "Try Mrs McKenna. I lent her one last week."

Should I return from all her ports of call empty handed, she would be in a foul mood for the rest of the day, taking it out on me for not having been successful in my errand.

Of course, life wasn't entirely unrelieved gloom. Sometimes when Mom was flush she'd treat us to the cinema, and I had many long discussions with Dad about football, which we both loved, but what I felt most acutely in my daily life, I suppose, was the lack of any adult I could really admire and look up to for help, guidance and as a pattern for my own life. All around me I saw not only youngsters all too ready to settle for the working class grind, but also adults crushed by poverty and ignorance. No-one saw a life beyond what they had, no-one saw me as a person worth getting to know, and as I looked into the future all I could see was a featureless plain of misery, from which I became increasingly desperate to escape.

The only islands of pleasure in all this misery were the few precious holidays I had during my childhood. I only ever had four breaks away from

Birmingham, two with my parents and two with my grandparents. I never quite made the promised trip to Holt Fleet but just after the war, when Butlin's opened their Skegness camp, Gran, Grandad, Aunt Maud, Reggie and I went off to sample the delights of a holiday camp. It looked still very much like a war-time army camp, but some cheerful paint and pretty gardens gave it a festive air. The chalets were spartan, the food institutional, for rationing was still very much in force, but what fun we had. We ate our plain food off long trestle tables with no cloths, just like school dinners, and Reggie and I had our own little chalet with two bunk beds, the top one of which was reached by an exciting ladder. Much to my satisfaction I got to sleep in the top bunk because Reggie, who had claimed it on the first night as senior member, fell out of it three times on the first night and thereafter prudently decided that it would be safer to sleep nearer the ground. Anyway, Reggie went down with a throat infection just after we got there and had to spend a couple of days in the sick bay, but apart from that we had a great time, riding strange bicycles made for two, swimming, falling into the boating lake and spending the evenings being entertained, either in the camp theatres or in the ball-room where famous dance bands played for us. My aunt was much impressed at getting the autograph of Nat Temple, the famous bandleader, but since I'd never heard of him I was less impressed. After the excitement of our first holiday, indeed our first trip out of Birmingham, we had the infinite pleasure of the journey home on a steam train, the regular rhythm of the wheels over the tracks playing a thrilling tune that kept us enthralled for the whole journey, for we'd never travelled on any sort of conveyance that could be compared to this.

When I was about 13, and recovering from a broken toe, which had necessitated plaster up to the knee, my grandparents took me on a holiday with them to Bournmouth, to stay in a little boarding house, as convalescence after my illess, so they told my parents. The place we stayed in was kept by a quiet little woman, who greeted us every morning as we came into the dining room for breakfast with the words: "Good morning, Mr. and Mrs. Nash, and Brenda.", but I was too pleased to be there to be aggrieved at sounding like something of an afterthought! I swam in the rough sea, mooched about the souvenir shops where I bought my mother a teapot of monumental ugliness, in the shape of an odd, orange-coloured thatched cottage, and, one afternoon when it rained, Grandad took us to the cinema, to see Danny Kaye in "Knock on Wood". I had a whole week when

I could choose what we did, and I revelled in it. Once again, I had reason to be grateful to my loving grandparents.

I only ever had two holidays with my parents. Once, as a teenager, I returned to Butlin's at Skegness. The camps were still organised like schools: I played netball for my house. There was, this time, no hideously cheerful voice to raise us from our slumbers at some unearthly hour of the morning with the greeting: "Good morning, campers!" but the famous redcoats were just as determinedly eager to make us enjoy ourselves as they had been when I'd gone there just after the war. I swam, I roller-skated, I was coached in table-tennis by an international player, I played football, and made a host of friends, many of whom I wrote to for some years afterwards.

My only other holiday came in 1958, just before I went off to university. Reggie had just finished his National Service in the army, having served in Cyprus during the EOKA emergency, and my parents decided that he must have a holiday on his return. One week in August duly found us, in a huge ex-army bell-tent, which reminded me of pictures of old scout camps, presided over by Baden Powell himself, digging trenches in the sodden ground to try to prevent ourselves from being washed away by the torrential downpours which we endured for virtually the whole week. Still, we gritted our teeth, and enjoyed Paignton Zoo, the beach, Goodrington Sands and my father and Reggie even patched up their feud long enough to share a drink at the nearest pub.

At home, something occurred in 1953 that would take us out of our dreary existence and unite, once again, the whole community in celebration, in a way that hadn't happened since the war – the coronation of Elizabeth II. Never since the end of the war had there been such celebrations. For the first and last time, the people from both ends of the road came together, and meetings were held to decide just what form our communal celebrations were to take, and how it was all to be paid for. Once more, scraps of material were salvaged to make bunting and old Union Jacks were fished out from junk holes and refurbished in a frenzy of nationalistic zeal, and we listened for weeks on the radio to details of how other communities across the country planned to spend the great day. Every gramophone and radio set blared out the great sentimental hit tune of the time:

"In a golden coach is a heart of gold,

A Pocket With A Hole

Driving through old London town."

As the big day approached, little Union Jacks were made for the children to wave, though quite what at wasn't very clear, and we prepared to wear clothes of patriotic red, white and blue. I was absolutely horrified to discover that my mother had bought from one of the clothing reps, the most incredibly ugly red, white and blue dress for me to wear. It was a geometric patterned affair, with a huge circular skirt, which was far too long for me. At the neck was a a cheap mock cameo brooch, bearing a poor likeness of the Queen upon it. Suddenly, the day lost some of its magic for me as I contemplated this monstrosity, but my mother insisted on my wearing it.

We planned a programme of events, races for the children, a fancy dress competition, and other events, and we waited in a state of great excitement for the day to come. It had never entered our heads that on the wonderful day the sun wouldn't shine, after all it was June, and the weather wouldn't dare not co-operate, would it? After all, anything less than perfect weather would be tantamount to treason, wouldn't it? But it rained, all the same. The races went on in a veritable deluge. A conference amongst the organisers led to the decision that it would be dangerous for the girls to run in such conditions, so our races were changed, to my infinite disgust, to walking races. However, my rather ruffled pride was somewhat mollified by my winning one of the races and gaining as my prize a rather smart green handbag.

I had not been intending to compete in the fancy dress competition, but our next-door neighbours insisted that I do so, for, with their theatrical background, they just loved dressing up. They decided that I should go as "Miss Correspondence 1953". An old dress was covered completely with letters, telegrams and post-cards, carefully saved by the girls from work; a head-dress was made from envelopes, bearing the words "Miss Correspondence" round the front, rather like the paper hats you got from the seaside, bearing cheeky messages such as "Kiss me quick!" Round my wrists I wore bracelets of paper-clips. Unfortunately, by the time the judges came to judge the competition, many of the costumes, thanks to the rain, were very second-hand looking, indeed. Those children who had unwisely chosen skimpy costumes – the babies in nappies and Hawaiian dancers in grass skirts – were half-frozen in the cold, and their grass skirts dripped icy rainwater down their legs. The make-up of the pirates and gypsies ran in streaks down their faces, making them look more like coal miners, and the knight in armour, who had looked so splendid in his silver cardboard suit, was reduced to tears as his armour collapsed into a heap of soggy mush. I, however, was triumphant, and to my neighbours' great pleasure, I won first prize – a brush, comb and mirror set, with a regal picture of our new queen on the back.

It was impossible to eat the celebration tea out of doors: it was too wet. Luckily, a room had been hired in a local school, just in case, and, to my disappointment, we ate indoors, squelching over the parquet floor, leaving little pools of dirty water everywhere we went.

In the evening the weather relented somewhat and a gramophone was carried into the street for dancing. The children watched the adults making fools of themselves, stepping on each other's feet, getting the steps wrong and giving us, as the evening wore on, lots of innocent amusement, as they drank more, and became less steady on their feet during the dancing. Somehow, Tony managed to get drunk and while imprudently trying to get upstairs to the bathroom, fell down the stairs and lay in a comotose heap in the hall, while a group of us looked on from the doorway. We summoned several adults to his assistance, but as they were in little better condition than Tony himself, their attempts to carry him upstairs only led to his mother's discovering, when she returned home from the party, an untidy heap of bodies cluttering up her hall.

Finally, the children were all packed off to bed, leaving the adults to reflect that Westcott Road had done the new queen proud, and many of them were reminded of the last great celebrations after the end of the war, and the hopes they'd all had then. Now, they looked forward to a new Elizabethan age. I, however, with all the cynicism of my 13 years, thought tomorrow would be just as awful as all the days that preceded it, and, of course, I was right.

All too soon, our family would be broken up for good. Gran would be forced to sell her house and Reg would move out when I went off to university, to live first back at home, in response to my father's plea to forget their feud, and then into a bed-sitter in Moseley. I, after university, would never live back home again.

CHAPTER 10

Secondary School

I had hated Primary School: in Miss Brookes's lessons I had closed my eyes, clenched my fists and prayed for the lesson to end and deliver me from torture, so when, at the tender age of ten, with very little primary education behind me, I went to Waverley Grammar School, I had no real hopes of liking that any better. I was the only child on our estate to go to a Grammar School: the other children all went to the local Secondary Modern, except for Reggie and a couple of other boys in our road, who went at 13+ to the Technical School to study engineering. For many years I was to be the only child on the estate to go to a Grammar school: I was to be in the sixth form before another girl in our road passed the ll+ and her

Waverley Grammar School

mother came to see me so that I could explain to her all about the system and what her daughter could expect. For a long time I was something of a fair-ground attraction to the neighbours: after all, I stayed on at school until I was eighteen, I learnt Latin and spoke French. They used to get me to say a few words of French to them, while they oohed and aahed at it, looking at me with the fascination one usually reserves for an exhibit in a freak show. When I went away to university they used to enquire of my mother, "How's your Bren getting on at school?" in tones that left no doubt of their opinion of people who needed still to be at school at such an advanced age.

At the age of ten, when I ventured into the unknown world of Grammar School, I was still a very nervous child, frightened of everything and everybody, terrified of every new place, and I approached my first day at my new school with all the joy of an aristocrat on his way to the guillotine. As the school was a long way from my home I went by bus, perching uncomfortably on the edge of the seat, clutching my new school satchel, which contained nothing more than a pen, pencil and ruler, mortally afraid that I'd miss my stop and get lost. I was terrifed that the other children would be posh and would sneer at my accent and I walked up the road behind little knots of fellow pupils with a marked feeling of doom. I was marginally reassured to hear that they spoke in much the same way as I did myself, but, to my unspeakable horror, I saw that they were all dressed differently from myself.

I had only been allowed to take the 11+ exam because my Gran had promised to buy me the uniform if I passed. In those days Grammar Schools were rather elite places, whose uniforms could only be bought from one very posh, exclusive, snooty (and fiendishly expensive) shop in Birmingham – The Don. I only ever went into this bastion of privilege once in my life, to buy an overpriced gym blouse when I was a sixth-former, but in the early days I'd never even heard of such a place. Neither my parents nor I had the remotest idea about school uniforms; indeed, we didn't really even know the names of all the schools. I'd only chosen Waverley because a girl I knew lived opposite a girl who was a pupil there, which flimsy reason had prompted me to sit for the school. I knew the school colours were navy blue and green, but beyond that I was totally ignorant. My Gran, who bought the uniform, could only afford it by using her club cheque from work, which was only cashable at a few shops, and assumed that what I would need would be an old-fashioned pleated gymslip (since made famous by the girls of St Trinian's), a navy blazer and a white blouse. She was right about the blazer and blouse, but wrong about the gymslip. So it was that I spent my schooldays, sticking out from my fellows like the proverbial sore thumb, in gymslips of a byegone age, while they wore up-to-the-minute four-gore pinafore dresses. To my over-sensitive mind I stood out alarmingly from all the rest and every Sunday I endured the agonising ritual of sewing in the box pleats on my increasingly shabby-looking gymslip and pressing them in, ready for school the next day. I was the only child in the school who wore the wrong uniform and I went through agonies of mortification all through my schooldays because of it. When once my mother made me go to school in a green blazer that someone had given her, when all the rest of the children wore navy, I thought I would die of shame and embarrassment. She said offhandedly, "It'll do. Green's a school colour, isn't it?" and she dismissed the subject from her mind while I sat in school assembly, a patch of alien green in a sea of navy blue, and wanted to die.

Even in the sixth form my embarrassment was not over. Although by this time we wore plain navy skirts instead of pinafore dresses, I never seemed to have the right thing. Once when I was preparing to attend

A group of sixth formers, 1956

Speech Day, where I was to receive a prize, I was desperate to find a skirt that would be suitable, the only remotely acceptable one having come to grief up against Mom's newly-painted kitchen wall, which had transformed a great chunk of it from blue to bilious green. My mother, appealed to in desperation for help, rummaged through the enormous chest of drawers in the front bedroom and unearthed a crumpled black skirt, with two huge and very conspicuous patch pockets on the front. She carelessly waved away my protests that it wouldn't do at all with the advice to remove the pockets, whereupon no-one would ever notice that it was black rather than blue. Realising that no further assistance would be forthcoming from that particular quarter, and with the ceremony only two hours away, I was forced to take her advice. I removed the pockets, as instructed, only to find, to my horror, that the dust of ages had been lodged in them, which left two large, only too obvious white lines outlining where the pockets had been. With time fast running out, I inked over the offending white lines with black ink, and prayed that no-one would notice. I went up on the stage to receive my prize, and it was only after I sat down again that I noticed great black inky patches on my hands, where I had rested them in my lap while waiting my turn to go up on the stage. The ink had not had time to dry and so I ended the evening looking more like a black and white minstrel than a serious student collecting an academic prize!

It wouldn't be too much of an exaggeration to say that my lack of regulation school uniform was to be a source of real anguish to me through the whole of my school career. The Senior Mistress, Miss Haworth, seemed to me to be a real Lucifer, put on this earth solely to be a source of torment to me. She constantly complained about my lack of school uniform, while I stood, red-faced, squirming with embarrassment. It took me back to all the horrors of Primary School where every day our finger nails were inspected to see that they were clean, and our handkerchieves had to be produced to prove that we had remembered to bring one. The trouble was I never had one: indeed, I didn't own one, and I lived in fearful dread of this morning ritual where I would be found, once again, to be wanting.

What I longed to tell Miss Haworth, but, being a cringing coward, never had the nerve, was that I would certainly wear the correct uniform if I could, since to be without it caused me so much grief, but since it was not in my power to change the situation, she'd do everyone a favour if she'd apply to my parents instead of making my life a misery. I was only too well aware that my school tie was the wrong one, bought in a second-hand clothes shop on my way back from one of my forays to the pawn shop – a tie of the right colours, but with stripes too narrow to deceive Miss Haworth's eagle eye; and that my cardigans, knitted by my Gran, were either too enormously capacious for my skinny frame or embellished with eccentric borders of green and navy, Gran's latest experiment in brightening up the dreary uniform. Indeed, I was only too conscious of what a rag-bag I looked. My blazer had a rather obvious hole in one of the pockets, my beret was virtually threadbare and bore a badge ragged at the edges where it had been chewed by the dog, my school coat was of any colour, style and age that I could manage to come by, and once I was reduced even to cutting off the tails from one of my father's white shirts in order to make myself a white blouse that would do for school. The worst of it all was that I couldn't even just brazen it out, and pretend to my fellow pupils that I was just some dangerous rebel, determined to do her own thing and the devil be damned. I hadn't the confidence for that: I just wanted to be unnoticed, the same as everybody else, an unremarkable part of the corporate body and to be otherwise made my life a real pain.

In our first year, we were arranged in classes according to our ll+ scores and I found myself in the top form, the 'A' form, where I stayed for the rest of my school career, even though after the first year we were rearranged into forms according to the results of our end of year exams. We were expected to uphold the traditions of the grammar schools and to walk with pride about the solid Victorian building, with its great tower and Gothic windows, a veritable cathedral, built to extol the virtues of Victorian philanthropy. Inside the school, the solid shabbiness echoed the public schools, as did the organisation. We were divided up into four 'houses', named, with appropriate scholarship, after the Waverley novels of Sir Walter Scott: Pirates, Ivanhoe, Redgauntlet and Talisman, whose colours were black, blue, red and yellow, respectively. Actually, the grand plan rather backfired here. As we walked round the school, its walls emblazoned with the usual long, boring, faded pictures of groups of scholars of the past, we were startled to see, only five years after the ending of the war, photos of pre-war students, all smiling, healthy and happy, neat in their navy pinafores but all sporting on the shoulder of their tunics, badges, from which glared the swastika. It was like coming across advertisements for the Hitler Youth, an impression not helped by the clipped moustache of Mr.

Wilde, who sat in the front centre of each group, which gave him an uncanny, if unfortunate, resemblance to Hitler himself. It appeared, as we were informed by an embarrassed teacher, that the logo for Talisman house had been, before the war, the ancient symbol that Hitler was all too soon to annex as his own, obliging the school to hurriedly change the logo to that of General de Gaulle's Cross of Lorraine.

I soon settled into doing what was expected of me, defending the honour of the school against the marauding hordes of the Oldknow Road Secondary Modern school on the bus home, trying to prevent our school berets from being cast carelessly from the windows of the top deck and untying our ties from the handrails of the bus, hopefully before we'd passed our stop, and trying to cope with a plethora of new teachers and new subjects.

There were, of course, still lessons that reduced me to a quivering jelly. As in Primary School, these were not so much the academic subjects but the 'extras'. Firstly, there was needlework, the subject that had caused me so much trouble in Primary School. I was much intimidated, for a start, by the teacher, the formidable Mrs. Harley, and I found sewing our cookery apron, to be put to use in our second year, an impossible task. Shades of the dreaded Miss Brookes began to close upon me as I vainly tried to sew an apron that would be even remotely wearable, and when I signally failed to extract the money from my uncaring parents to pay for the material, in spite of many requests, my misery was complete. In the end, the school stopped asking for payment and the subject was forgotten by everyone but me. My misery, however, went on, for the latter part of the first year, after the aprons were (more or less) finished, was given over to the making of a pair of navy blue gym knickers. Something went drastically wrong with my measurements somewhere along the line and my finished knickers were positively enormous. They reminded me of a cover for a medium-sized barrage balloon, they were so enormously capacious. They were, of course, no possible use to me, and they mouldered away in a junk cupboard at home, before finally vanishing both from sight and mind.

I had started school going on two buses, but it wasn't long, of course, before it was made clear to me that money was too short for me to spend so much on bus fares. I was, in truth, most aggrieved about this because, as I lived more than three miles away from the school I was entitled to receive travelling expenses from the council. These expenses were paid by money order each term. This money, of course, just found its way into Mom's purse and I was told to find a cheaper method of getting to school. I was thus obliged to walk over a mile up to the Coventry Road, where I got a bus to Small Heath, where I walked through the park to school. This journey I was to do throughout my school career, apart from the short time when I tried the experiment of going to school on Reggie's bike.

I stayed at school for lunch, taking school dinners, which, although the other children complained constantly about them, were my only decent meal of the day. When, in the sixth form, it was fashionable to decry school dinners and I gave them up to be with my friends, I much regretted it secretly, for my mid-day meal from then on consisted of a couple of pieces of bread and butter, brought from home, with the addition of a banana or a couple of portions of cheese spread, if I had money enough to buy it, or just bread and butter if I didn't, and a hot meal would have been welcome.

I went to school for eight years (1950–58) without much enthusiasm, did my maths homework on the bus, with the help of my friend, who was a mathematician, and just did what I was told at school, making myself as inconspicuous as possible. I was really grateful that none of the teachers, if they knew of my background, patronised me by making allowances for my straightened circumstances. I was treated the same as everyone else, expected to come up to the same standards, and I was glad. I could not under-achieve and blame my family background for my failure: I was expected to do what everyone else did, and I did it. This hard philosophy enabled me to get out of my poor background, go to university, at a time when only one working-class girl in five hundred had a university education, and so to make myself a different life.

After the first year and our sorting out by the exams, for a reason I have never fathomed, the academically clever, in the 'A' stream, did arts subjects, with the addition of Latin or German, while the next class, the 'S' form concentrated on science and the two equal 'B' forms just did a general curriculum. Why the brightest did arts and the less bright did science I just don't know, but the policy led to some odd results. I ended up at 'O' level with no science subject but maths, and my friend, who was to read Maths at university, had no Physics or Chemistry and was forced to do Geography at 'A' level, to go with her Maths. How quaint the restricted syllabus seems now, in these days of a wide curriculum! My son has eleven 'O' levels, ranging from Music, three languages, Physics,

Chemistry and Maths, whereas in my day even the brightest child did only eight subjects, within rigidly defined limits.

When it became necessary for us to choose between Art, Domestic Science or Music, I was faced with a real dilemma. I couldn't do Music because I didn't play an instrument; I couldn't face Domestic Science and the forceful Mrs. Harley, so, and in spite of my singular lack of talent for the subject, I opted for Art, but, after a couple of years of effort on the part of our Art teacher, Mr. Davies, I was advised to admit defeat and give up the subject. As our form teacher was also our English teacher, I thus spent art afternoons doing extra English alone, which, strangely enough, proved to be a blessing in disguise, because, under the kind and expert tuition of Mrs. Boot, I became very good at English.

I coped adequately with most academic subjects, although I still could not do arithmetic, and life in the classroom was unremarkable. Being an arts dominated class we were most unevenly distributed with regard to sex, for there were 22 girls in the class to only 7 boys, which made for a quieter life, I suppose. The teachers were, for the most part, very strict. Our French teacher, Mr. Mills, was totally ferocious: I thought of him every time we sang the words of Blake in assembly about 'those dark, satanic mills', but he was an excellent teacher, and under his expert tuition I thrived. The teachers, clad in their academic gowns, swept about the school, gowns flying out behind them, like Count Dracula. There were, of course, teachers whom we knew we could torment with impunity and, thanks to my no doubt most reprehensible habit of listening to 'The Goon Show' during Miss Christopher's Geography lessons, I was to fail my 'O' level Geography, mainly as a result of a map of the North East of England which resembled nothing on the face of this earth. However, we were the top class, after all, and we were generally taught by the most senior staff, whom we generally (if not in Geography) rewarded for their efforts by decent 'O' level results.

For much of my school years I simply did as I was told, in the same spirit of resignation bred in me first in hospital and then in Primary School. I never quite was able to stop my heart from giving an uncomfortable lurch every time I heard Miss Haworth's super-refined tones, calling to me in a deceptively quiet tone that echoed the length of the corridor, "Brenda, come here. I want a word". And once more, that detector of all abuses would graphically describe to me my shortcomings. It came as something of a relief to me to hear her berating some other unfortunate instead of me, in her carefully modulated tone of delicate reproach: "Elizabeth! Find yourself something better to do. I have just been marking your Geography examination and your knowledge of industrial India was meagre in the extreme." And, her dissatisfaction duly demonstrated, she glided silently up the staircase to her study like a rather substantial wraith.

For many years I crept reluctantly to school in the morning, wondering gloomily just what detail of my dress or behaviour would be singled out for criticism that day, and squirmed uncomfortably every time it was my turn to read the lesson on the stage in morning assembly, for I'd be only too miserably conscious of her eyes boring into my back as I read, anxiously looking for some other fault to find. So, as time went on, school became more and more of an alien place to me where I didn't really belong.

Most of the social life in our teenage years, for most of my schoolfriends at least, centred round school. Indeed, many girls married boys they'd met at school. My own social life, such as it was, centred around the cinema and trips to the swimming bath with Reggie. I met boys at home; even fell in love a couple of times with boys on holiday with relations on the estate. When a family round the corner had a Canadian cousin to stay, the pace of life picked up a bit, as did the heartbeat of all the local girls, for he was devastatingly handsome. We all went swimming, in a group and to the cinema, but I, to my disappointment, just remained one of the crowd, but at least the handsome Canadian had filled a niche in my fantasy life for a little while!

The social and sexual code was very strict. Sex was a subject of which I was only too well aware, of course, but only in the sense of the problems it tended to bring to men and women, in the form of marital disharmony and unwanted pregnancy. My mother once attempted to explain 'the facts of life' to me , with singularly little success, since her own knowledge of the subject was at best hazy and at worst inaccurate. Her attempts at explaining menstruation included most alarming references to "bad blood, that has to come away" intimating that should this fail to occur, dire, if unspecified, consequences would ensue, and her explanation of where babies came from (having had first-hand experience of it herself) was a good deal more convincing than her attempt at explaining how they got there in the first place (though, of course, she'd also had first-hand experience of that, as well!)

Boys and girls at school entered into relationships, of course, but there was no free and easy attitude to sex. Indeed, it was not uncommon for boys to have restrictions on how late they could stay out at night, just as much as girls. In the fifth year, one of the girls, in an attempt to climb over a gate so that they could get to the bus-stop in time for her date to get his bus home, to meet his parents' deadline for when he had to be in, split her tight, (and she'd hoped, so seductive) skirt from hem to waist, in a frantic attempt to scale the gate in time!

This sort of story was retailed to me at school, for I had no social contact with any of my schoolfriends, apart from my friend Edna, whom I had known in Primary School and with whom I went to and from school every day. Part of the reason for this isolation was that we all came from widely differing areas of Birmingham, and further afield, but also because I had no desire to invite my schoolfriends home and let them see the chaos in which we lived. Every morning I rose at crack of dawn, got up my younger sisters, fed them, made sure they were washed and dressed, took the younger one over the road to Jessie Butler, who minded her while Mom was at work, then I abandoned the house, dirty crockery, clutter and dirt, and set off on my long journey to school. As soon as I got home from school, I had to try to restore some order and decorum into Babel, clearing up the mess and clutter in the living room, collecting the dirty crockery from all round the house, where teacups had just been abandoned by the adults the night before, clean out the ashes from the grate, lay and light a new fire and then begin to prepare and cook my father's dinner, for when he came home from work. My sisters and I ate what we could find to eat, sitting in the kitchen while I kept an eye on my father's cooking meal. The sleaziness of the house, always looking as if it had been gone through by a particularly inefficient burglar, was a sight I was not anxious for my schoolfriends to see, and since I didn't have the money to frequent the places they went to in the evenings, nor any of the fashionable clothes or up-to-date hairstyles that they took for granted, we never met outside school.

Actually, fashion was very important in the 1950s, not just because of a reaction to the dreariness and austerity of the war years, but because the '50s was the age of the teenager. Up until then, children had dressed like little adults. Boys wore jackets and grey flannels like their fathers, with a sober suit for Sundays, just like scaled-down versions of adults. Girls graduated from childish ribbons and flowered dresses to being mirror-images of their mothers. Then, in the 1950s, when rationing and austerity were finally swept away, and Harold MacMillan was telling us, with some justification "you've never had it so good", advertisers turned their attention to the new consumers, with money to spend and ripe for exploitation – the teenagers. To the consternation and blank incomprehension of their parents, young people, pushed into anarchy and degeneration (so their parents said) by the bursting upon their incredulous ears of Elvis Presley's "Heartbreak Hotel" and the sheer exuberance of Bill Haley's "Rock around the Clock", began to try deliberately to set themselves apart from their elders. In came crew cuts, long, greasy, D.A. cuts, the Tony Curtis look and clothes that sent their parents into paroxysms of horror – flourescent bobby sox, full skirts, worn over layers of petticoats, elastic belts, pony tails for the girls; draped lapels, velvet collared jackets, drainpipe trews and thick, crepe-soled shoes for the boys, coupled with an abandoned style of dancing that left their elders clucking disapprovingly about moral turpitude and predicting disaster. So important did teenage fashions become in the national psyche, even comedians made jokes about them:

"Doctor, I have water on the knee."
"Well wear drainpipes, then!"

and many an incredulous adult swallowed hard on seeing a Teddy boy, resplendent in bright pink suit with black velvet collar. One uninitiated shop assistant, on seeing a boy come in wearing a jacket in the latest tear-drop material asked innocently "Oh, is it raining outside?"

No doubt, the spirit of teenage rebellion was about: James Dean saw to that. But not in me. My only concession to the newly liberated teen-age fashions was an elastic belt that Mom had finally grudgingly bought for me. Not for me the sitting in coffee bars, a moustache of froth on my upper lip where I had plunged into the beige cloud of froth on my espresso coffee, the latest drink, spewed out from an Italian machine, which hissed alarmingly and belched out steam, and with more levers than a signal box. I continued to go nowhere in particular, wearing a pair of shoes and clothes borrowed from Mom and longed to be part of this new world, where people actually took notice of what teenagers thought, dreamed or wanted from life.

As for school, I couldn't even gain any much needed kudos on the sports field, for school teams played on Saturday mornings, when I was busy with my household chores. My only concession to school activities lay in the choir, which I loved. Our school was not much noted for great academic achievement, but it was noted for its music. During my years at the school, we produced one opera star, a pop group with hits to its name ('The Ivy League') and a member of the famous Ian Campbell Folk Group. The school also boasted a fine French choir, good enough to broadcast on radio. I cherished a secret ambition to be asked to join this choir, which was a great honour, but in the meantime, under the expert tuition of Mr. Walker, the school choir went from strength to strength. We practised every lunchtime, we gave concerts and Mr Walker cashed in on the wealth of singing talent in the school to compose operas to showcase the voices he had to choose from. With music by Mr. Walker and librettos by Mr. Barnes, the history master, the school operas became quite famous in Birmingham, and brought the school much good publicity. I was never in the operas myself, for I couldn't raise the bus fare to attend the many rehearsals necessary, but I have remained forever grateful for the world of music that was offered to me by being in the choir. Through this, I became familiar with the works of famous composers and became part of the mainstream of classical music, performing works by the classical composers, as well as being well versed in the English tradition of folk songs and the world of Negro Spirituals. It was a legacy for which I am even now grateful.

Years later, when I was on a visit to the school, I was quite dumbfounded by having Mr. Walker say casually to me, "You know, I always wanted you to join the French choir, but somehow I never got round to asking you," leaving me to ponder on what might have been. What a boost it would have been to my all too fragile morale! But then I reflected that I'd never have been able to raise the bus fare to go to rehearsals and to our numerous engagements, so I sensibly reasoned that perhaps it had all been for the best.

We came up to our fifth year at school, our 'O' level year, but there were no outward signs of increased activity. 'O' levels were just another part of school life, and we took them in our stride. Anyway, we had a most delicious distraction to push the thought of exams deep into the background. A new boy arrived as a temporary member of our class. He came from India and was called Wally Hammond (a name redolent of the great age of English cricket) and he was the most handsome boy any of us had ever seen: perfect profile, the figure of a Greek god, and a permanent tan. We all knew, of course, that he would soon become the personal property of the siren of the fifth year and, indeed, so it proved. How could the rest of us hope to compete against a girl brought up to be beautiful by a glamorous and elegant mother, who called her children outlandish names like Eithne and Vaughan? What chance had we Brendas, Shirleys and Sheilas against that sort of exoticism!

The rather sedate pattern of relations between the sexes that I saw at school, with a great deal of talk about sex, but very little action, was certainly not repeated at home in the more rough and tumble atmosphere of a working-class housing estate , and even I had the same sorts of experiences we've all had at some time in our teenage years, of being manhandled by callow youths, anxious to improve their technique of French kissing (and reminding me invariably and disgustingly in their botched attempts, of a vacuum cleaner!) and increase their practical knowledge of human anatomy at the same time. I soon learnt a good practical technique of shin-kicking, which preserved me from too much harm, and turned my attention to older men, whose education in such matters is more complete!

Our local group of the sexually curious (or rather, obsessed) centred round Tony and his sidekicks, Sniffer and Bongo, along with various other of the local boys who drifted in and out of the gang. Their aim in life, as is that of all teenage boys, centred on the paramount need for enlightening sexual experience (they were not at all fussy about what or where). They tried as an opening gambit climbing on the roof of the ladies' lavatories at the local cinema, and peering through the skylight at the assembled ladies as they went about their business but, totally disappointed at just how little feminine flesh is revealed in such circumstances, they withdrew, disgruntled, to try their luck nearer home.

Their attention settled, not surprisingly, on the local beauty, a rather fey girl called June, with long dark hair and the considerable inconvenience of a loathsome spoilt brat of a younger brother who her parents insisted accompanied her everywhere, which considerably reduced the opportunities for high jinks. Her every movement was monitored by her revolting sibling, who clung to her like the Old Man of the Sea, and reported on her every action to her parents. In view of this considerable impediment she remained, rather frustratingly for all concerned, virginally untouched, even by Tony, who lived next door to her. In desperation the gang turned to other girls from different estates and dark tales reached my ears of unseemly goings on on the piece of waste ground over behind the shops. Irene, who lived a few doors from me, pointed an accusing finger one day at a girl from another estate, averring that she had permitted Tony "to do dirty things to her, over behind the shops" but just what evil deeds had been perpetrated were not specified, out of deference, I suppose, to my delicate Grammar School sensibilities. Sniffer told lurid tales of three in a bed activities in his house while his mother was at work, stories no doubt somewhat embellished but which I could well believe, since he played truant from school for months on end. His mother dispatched him every morning with his books and sandwiches, then she went off to work, leaving him to conveniently forget to go to school and to spend the day in more congenial activities. In the end, in desperation, he was coerced by his parents to join the Merchant Navy, where he could roam the world and be no further trouble to them.

As time went on Tony became quite obsessed with tearing June from her intrusive brother long enough to have his wicked way with her, so much so that desperation led him to hatch a plot which, although not without its farcical side, might well have had most serious consequences. June, Irene and I were standing, as usual, on the patch of green at the corner of the road, talking and throwing a tennis ball to each other in a desultory way, waiting for something to happen, when we were approached by Tony, Bongo and Brian, a quiet dark-haired boy who lived in the next street. They insinuated themselves into the ball game, stealing the ball from us and involving us in a chase to try to get it back. I was puzzled by this; they seemed to be making an effort to manoeuvre us down to the other end of the street, but why, I had no idea. It was obvious to me that the boys were up to something and I advised the girls not to play along with their game but just to let them have the ball and go home. They, however, seemed determined to go with the boys and find out what was going on. Before we knew it we found ourselves in a secluded piece of the waste ground behind the shops, and I knew we'd been lured into a trap.

We were soon to know what the game was; they'd planned it all very carefully beforehand. June, it appeared, was to offer Tony, or at least be forced to give, what he'd been wanting for so long. Without more ado, completely ignoring the inconvenient presence of Irene and myself, June was manhandled to the ground. It was a most clumsy and unedifying assault. Brian, appalled at the reality of the fantasy they'd discussed in such titillating detail beforehand, with such lip-smacking relish, stood by, ashamed and embarrassed, while Irene and I, in a sort of frozen cameo of shock and amazement at the crassness of it all, watched while an unseemly melee took place on the ground. All that was gained in the way of sexual gratification was a fleeting touch of the much desired breasts, which Bongo obtained by the crude process of thrusting his hand down her blouse, while Tony held her down and she kicked and screamed, cursing like a fishwife. Irene and I, finally awoken from our shock, laid into the boys with fists and feet, and they were finally obliged to give up the attempt. By the time Sniffer arrived to join in the fun it was to a scene of breathless, red-faced youngsters, all in a state of some disarray, and Bongo boasting about his pathetic triumph.

There was nothing to do but to gather our scattered wits and go home, thinking that if June and Irene couldn't see that they were being led into a trap, they'd get into even more trouble before they were much older and all of us surveying the mud and grass stains on our clothes and wondering how we were going to explain them away to our parents. None of us ever mentioned the incident again, even to each other, but I was disappointed to discover that from then on, whenever I met Brian in the street he greeted me with such embarrassment and red-faced shame that we could never become friends. It must be said, however, that in spite of all the attempts to force the pace of sexual enlightenment we all still seemed to live by the old adage, "Nice girls don't", for in spite of all Tony's efforts to change matters, no girl that I knew of ever got pregnant before marriage: they just didn't dare.

While I was in the sixth form, Reggie, who had by this time finished his apprenticeship at a little engineering firm in Bordesley Green, was obliged to go into the Army to do his National Service. He spent his final year in Cyprus, during the EOKA emergency. Actually he didn't seem to fight anyone very much, apart from a recalcitrant camel that is, but I liked to think of him as a war hero! His being away left me once more alone to carry the burden of the household. As a result of my having gained six mediocre passes at 'O' level I was now set fair for 'A' levels and then on to university, a prospect which, when I bothered to think about it, filled me with some alarm. But that was all in the distant future, and I had more immediate things to deal with. The iron had exploded into lurid blue flashes and little pieces, leaving me to go to school in school dresses that resembled a wrung out dishcloth, and face, once again, the barbs of Miss Haworth's disapproval. But, still, life went on.

Actually, life would have gone on a good deal less pleasantly and far more depressingly than it did had it not been for a most unexpected something that gave a lift to my miserable existence – football. Marx may well have been right when he averred that religion was the opium of the Russian people: for the English working classes, however, that role was definitely filled by football. Every working-class boy in my day played football all the time and dreamt of fame and fortune as he kicked a scuffed, worn rubber ball around the streets. We played football in the road, under the street lamp on dark winter evenings until late evening, using the thick line across the concrete road sections as a goal line and on Sundays we'd trek up to the local park to play with real goalposts on a real pitch, after the weekend matches were over and the pitches were reduced to acres of ankle-deep, clinging mud, more reminiscent of ploughed fields than sports fields. I, clad in tight skirt that made any sort of physical exertion difficult, would be in goal, hitching my inconvenient skirt up and tucking it into my knickers, which gave me the freedom to make spectacular saves. The rubber ball would be fired at me from all angles by all comers, and if I failed to reach it, it would cannon off crossbar or post, the velocity and spin of it reducing it to a small oval as it shot off to finish a long way away, where it was retrieved by a rather disgruntled small boy, who was only allowed to play if he fetched the ball for us. After the game, plastered in cloying mud, the glutinous substance adhering to my school shoes in such quantities as to give them the appearance of the weighted boots of the deepsea diver, I'd go home, hiding my shoes and my mud-spattered clothes from Mom until I'd had time to let the mud dry enough to allow it to be scraped off with a knife, revealing the shoe leather again.

I didn't play in a team, of course. It was to be another 40 years before girls were allowed to do that. I merely raged against a convention that allowed boys of no talent to play in teams but denied me the same right, purely because of an accident of birth. Not for the first time, I realised that to be born a girl was to be born a second-class citizen. And yet, in spite of my mother's hand wringing and anguish over a daughter who was "a real Tomboy" I didn't actually ever want to be a boy. Indeed, sexually, I've always rather enjoyed being female. What I wanted was the tacitly accepted, unspoken, superiority of the male in working-class society and the freedom that this status offered. Looking back now, of course, I can easily appreciate that for working-class boys life was just as closed in the end and just as circumscribed as it was for girls – a soul-destroying job in a factory, early marriage and the financial responsibilities of a wife and children, relieved only by trips to the pub with the boys at weekends, and football on Saturday afternoons. Not so very different, really, from the accepted lot of the girls – a couple of years after school working in a factory or a shop, then early marriage and the closing shutters of husband, children and making ends meet. What I did envy boys, however, was their unquestioned superiority within their society. Even in their teens they were superior to their female relations, even to their mother, for they bought in a wage, which gave them the right to be indulged by their mothers and treated like an equal by their fathers. They were something in their world: girls were nothing.

My interest in football started young. My father had been a fine player, having the chance to turn professional in his teens and when he managed to get a real leather football for Reggie I was thrilled. Reggie, quite atypically, had no interest in sport whatever, and I gleefully seized on the new football as my own prized possession. Instead of Reggie, it was I who became a goalkeeper, as my father had been, and discussed the finer points of the game with him. I took to the game, both as a spectator sport and as a philosophical concept, like the proverbial duck to water, and so began a love affair with the game and with its most gifted players, that has lasted all my life. No doubt sociologists and psychologists have all manner of clever theories to explain the hold the game has had over generations of poor working-class children – it isn't, in all truth, that hard to find. What football did for me, as for others, was to give an opportunity to people whose lives are dull, routine, penny-pinching and unfulfilling to live for a while every week in the glitter and excitement of monumental struggles for success in a fiercely partisan war where, along with your fellows, all conveniently advertised by the wearing of your team's colours, you can share for a while in glory, skill, achievement and a fame to which individually you have no hope of aspiring. The weekdays are one life:

dreary at best, heart-breakingly awful at worst – the weekends are something else entirely.

On matchdays I rose at dawn to get my chores done. I scrubbed the house from top to bottom, coaxing the weekday dust and grime out of everything. I shopped, washed, cooked and cleaned, then, with my pocket-money clinking encouragingly in my purse (7/6 a week if Dad could be reminded and cajoled into parting with so much), I'd make my way to the station to begin my journey to another world. Heavily disguised in my black and gold scarf (for, to my father's rage and chagrin, I supported, not his beloved Birmingham City, but the enemy, Wolverhampton), clad in a hideously patterned orange and black houndstooth check coat bought for me by my Gran (she went in for stomach-turning patterns – a large grey and white check affair followed the orange and black), I'd make for Wolverhampton and immerse myself in the pre-match atmosphere. Sometimes on the train I'd meet a group of men, fellow supporters, who took me under their wing, bought me food and paid my entrance fee to the match, which, in view of the permanently parlous state of my finances, was the equivalent of manna from heaven. When I didn't see my friends, I'd make for the sports shop kept by one of my footballing heroes, Jimmy Mullen, to try to get a few words with him before the match. Having ensured that he knew the importance of winning and thus confounding my father's prognostications on the outcome of the match, I'd then make for the ground, by this time thronging with supporters, all noisy, excited and cheerful, and take my place on the terraces in the seething phalanx of fellow devotees, a powerful solidarity based on a shared passion. In those days we happily shared our territory with visiting supporters, swapped programmes with them, frightened them with tales of our team's former exploits, held learned debates with them on the merits of their centre-forward (inferior, of course, to our own), or the shortcomings of their goalkeeper (ours, naturally, was beyond reproach), and prepared them for the soon to come trouncing their team was about to suffer.

After the match I haunted the players' car-park until the players emerged, so that I could get autographs and see at close quarters the heroes whose faces adorned the walls of my bedroom and stared at me from the pages of my lovingly-compiled scrapbooks, and whose grace and artistry haunted my dreams. Once I went triumphantly off to catch my train, crowing over having managed to get the autograph of the great Jackie

Wolves v Sheffield United, October 15th, 1955

Billy Wright

Milburn, of Newcastle and England fame, only for an uninitiated fool on the train to reduce me to speechless rage and incredulity by asking innocently, "Who's Jackie Milburn?"

I felt very jealous when Buster managed to come by a signed picture of Tom Finney; I duly despatched a photo to Blackpool to get the autograph of my first great football hero, Stanley Matthews, so it would be Buster's turn to be jealous. I basked in the reflected glory of my team's successes, and even now I know just how it feels when the deprived Liverpool youngster stands on the Kop, feeling that his team's successes are his own, for isn't he an infintessimal part, in his devotion and devout allegiance, of the legend that is Liverpool F.C.? I felt as if at last I belonged somewhere and I drank in the atmosphere on match days like a man in the desert quenching his thirst at an oasis. The team's successes were my triumphs: their defeats were my tragedy, too, and I went through the whole gamut of emotions every Saturday that were denied me expression in my dreary daily round.

Then, full of the wonders of the afternoon – yet another splendid goal by Roy Swinbourne, a miraculous save by Bert Williams, or a gem of pure artistry by Peter Broadbent; or suffering agonies of mortification of a defeat by Chelsea, of all awful teams, I'd take the train home, realising when I got there just how hungry I was, for pocket money didn't stretch to the match and food as well. All my pocket-money for a whole week gone, blown on this orgy of exploding emotions, I'd then have to rely on Bill,(the husband of Aunt Lizzie's Olive, who had moved in with my Gran after Grandad's death, to help finance her house), who could usually be inveigled into taking me in his car to mid-week games that I couldn't otherwise have afforded to attend. So often did I presume on his good nature and affection that his wife used to say, at least half-jokingly, "It's not every wife who'd cook her husband's supper when he's spent the evening with another woman!"

But of course Olive knew nothing of the thrill of Wolves v Borussia Dortmund or the exhilaration of Wolves v Valencia, or the fun of a Cup replay at St Andrew's, hanging from the girders at the back of the terracing, surrounded by a swaying blue and white sea of supporters, 63,000 of them, all lost in yet another life or death struggle.

For me, football was something of a saviour. Local people ribbed me good-naturedly about my team, gleefully prophesying doom and defeat, while I was confident of yet another marvellous victory: the local newsagent saved me marked-down books on football and even my mother was once sufficiently moved to buy for me a copy of 'Football Monthly' which contained a most covetable action picture of Stanley Matthews in full colour.

Having been forced, however reluctantly, to acknowledge that, owing to an accident of birth, I would never be allowed to play football for Wolves and England, I decided on the next best thing: if I couldn't get there by right, I'd have to do it by proxy – by marriage. After all, girls were supposed to have no other profession but marriage, weren't they? Although my own love-life was unremarkable to say the least, if not quite stagnant, I grandly decided that in my fantasy life I should have nothing but the best. Accordingly, I chose as the object of my devotion the captain of my team, as well as the captain of England – Billy Wright. Two birds with one stone – both Wolves and England with the same man. So it was that for years I waited patiently in the rain outside a multitude of football grounds in the hope of getting an autograph and a few words with my idol, while at night I lay in the dark, beneath my threadbare army blankets and dreamt of a different life: a life of glamour and glory (of reflected glory, to be sure, but glory all the same) and an end to misery and insignificance.

Needless to say, when Billy Wright married in 1958, to a woman with all the glamour I so conspicuously lacked, my heart fell into so many pieces that I'm not sure I've collected them all up even now, and, when he died in 1994 I wept tears such as I never wept for any of my now departed relatives.

What had gone out of my life was a hope, a promise, a sense of the attainable (a false hope, of course, and one which had always remained just out of reach, like a mirage shimmering tantalisingly in the heat of the desert) but one which had helped me to get through the toughest part of my life, my teenage years, and without which I would have been even more bereft.

I took my 'A' levels in 1957 at the age of 17 and, horrified at the thought of a summer at home, without even Reggie for comfort, persuaded my friend Edna that we should do the fashionable thing and go off to work at a hotel by the sea for the summer. Two schoolfriends, who were already fixed up, gave us an address in North Devon, and the beginning of July saw us on a train bound for Woolacombe, where we would be met by a car that would take us to Mortehoe, where we were to spend the rest of the summer. We had both bought hats for the occasion: concoctions out of the music-hall, bought at C & A and guaranteed to bring a smile to the face of even the most charitable beholder. Mine was a little black, head-hugging affair, with a long black feather which was all too prone to poke me inconveniently in the left eye, and Edna's was equally black, but large, flat, like a felt pancake, which perched insecurely on top of her luxuriant dark hair. If our new boss was surprised by our eccentric appearance, to her credit she was too polite to show it, and we soon settled into our new surroundings.

The work was very hard, with long hours, and only one half-day free a week. In the first week or so, before the season really got under way, we were given a whole day off, and I profited from it to take a sea trip from Ilfracombe to Lundy Island. After a two hour journey, we embarked into small boats for landing in the small harbour. It was an uncompromisingly vile day: the rain lashed down and the wind threatened to sweep us out to sea at every moment. The brave passengers struggled up the precipitate path that led from the beach to the top of the 200 foot high cliff, macs flapping in the breeze, wind whistling round them, arriving at the top bedraggled and exhausted. We spent what remained of our time ashore packed like sardines in the tiny pub on the top of the cliff, wet clothes steaming in the warm atmosphere, closed in behind windows streaming with condensation, until it was time to make the perilous descent of the track back to the boat. It had hardly been an enlightening experience: no puffins, no other seabirds for which the island was famous, just sheets of rain beating against the windows, and then a rough crossing back to Ilfracombe.

In those days, with so few people having cars, hotels offered their guests full board: breakfast, lunch, afternoon tea, then dinner at 8pm. This left us with a very hard routine. We rose at six and before 6.30 I would be brushing the stairs (no vacuuming in case I woke the guests) . After this we had our breakfast before serving breakfast to the guests. Two Swedish students had been engaged to wait at table: I and another girl were to be chamber maids, and Edna, with her 'O' level in Domestic Science, was to help with the cooking. After washing up after the guests' breakfast I departed to the bedrooms to do my duty as a chamber maid.

Lunch followed the cleaning of bedrooms and bathrooms. All the guests stayed for lunch. After this we had our own lunch: (whatever the guests had not chosen from the menu), washed up and then had some free time during the afternoon. Every third day it fell to me to prepare and serve afternoon tea, so I had to return before four o'clock and prepare trays of tea, bread and butter and scones for the guests to take tea in the lounge. Even on days when I was not preparing tea, I had only until 6pm to go into Woolacombe, go swimming or shopping, for I was in charge of children's suppers, and I had to prepare these at 6pm. Some small children did not dine with their parents at 8 o'clock, so I had to prepare suppers for them on a tray and take it to their rooms. I just had time to collect up the supper trays and then we were off again, preparing and serving dinner to the adult guests. This done, we were able to eat, wash up and finally call it a day. In the height of the season we would not be free until 10pm, which didn't leave much time to do anything else but go for a swim in the warm sea in the dark, or walk into Woolacombe to talk to the other students, working in different hotels from ourselves. We then, with the threat of another six o'clock start hanging over us, just slipped wearily into bed.

The only change to this hard routine came when we had a half day off, or on Sunday, when salad was served for lunch and no stair sweeping was permitted.

For working these very long hours we were paid £3 a week, plus our board and lodgings. I received tips from the guests, of course, sometimes as much as 10/- from a single guest, but often as little as 2/-. We were, however, well fed and well treated. We ate the same food as the guests, as much food as we wanted: it was rumoured that at some of the local hotels the staff had inferior food, nothing like what the guests ate, but I never found out whether it was true. The Devon air certainly seemed to do us good and Florrie, the Devon lady who called every morning to deliver the milk, commented on how much better we were looking after a few weeks of her native Devon air. We soon got to know all the local tradespeople, and our fellow workers, from the little lad who brought the morning papers (and rejoiced in the name of Winston), to the porter who came in every Saturday to carry the bags of arriving and departing guests. I saved a little of my unaccustomed wealth, unwisely sending a little home for my mother to keep for me, to buy a new skirt for school for the new term. Needless to say, I never saw the money again. The rest I prudently kept to spend on necessities; just as well, really, for I needed a new skirt, as I was to stay a third year in the sixth form, since I'd been only 17 when I'd taken my 'A' levels, which was considered too young to go to university.

Edna and I enjoyed our stay in Devon, notwithstanding the hard work, and her nearly chopping off her finger and gouging a deep hole in the palm of her hand, when the stem of a wineglass, which she was using to cut out scones, broke and stabbed her as neatly as a stiletto; and of my being scalded by boiling soup one day in the lunchtime rush. For some weeks we presented ourselves at the surgery of the local doctor to have our various wounds dressed. I was really sad when it came to the time to leave Devon and come back to Birmingham, and we drove to the station somewhat gloomily, taking as parting gifts from our employer alarm clocks set at the significant hour of 6am. Our employer had been very kind to us and her husband, who had recently retired from being a Major in the army, had made even piles of washing-up seem fun, with his endless tales of his life in the army.

We got back to school, to discover that I had been made Deputy Head

Girl. It was made clear to me by the retiring Head Girl that it was nothing but a sop to me, as senior pupil, and that I ought to have been Head Girl. I fully understood that I was considered not 'quite right' to be Head Girl, by virtue of my lack of school uniform and lack of the right background. Actually, although I did feel the slight, I didn't really much care: I hadn't expected anything. I'd been a prefect, of course, but most sixthformers were, since the sixth form in those days was quite small, but I hadn't given a thought to anything else. For one thing, I had other problems to contend with. Having gained good 'A' level grades the year before, and with the aim of studying French at university, I wanted to drop my third 'A' level subject, History, and take 'O' level German in a year, to give me a second modern language. Our silly option system at school had made us choose between Latin and German, and I'd had to take Latin, which in those days was an essential requirement for anyone wanting to read French at university. To my infinite rage, my Headmaster wouldn't hear of the plan. He had grandiose visions of my earning a State Scholarship (which were offered in those days by the Government for 'A' level results of high quality), for he saw the honour of the school as being at stake. With the stubbornness bred of years of adversity, I swore that if he made me take History again I would do no work in the subject and thus thwart his plans for the status-enhancing State Scholarship. So, all year I did no work in History, but, with the perversity of life I had come by this time to expect, my best mark was in History, and I won the prize for the subject for the second year running!

Actually, it was only in the sixth form that I won any prizes at all. I was, in fact, a very mediocre student. My friend, Edna, won prizes for academic excellence all the way through the school, from first year to fifth, though when I saw the stodgy books she won, Walter Scott novels of daunting length and other 'classics' that would, no doubt, remain unread, I didn't really much mind. Until the sixth form I had only ever once won a prize: in the first form, for spoken English. It seemed that all my acting, however reluctantly, in junior school plays had paid off at last, for, by reading aloud and reciting a poem I became the proud owner of a book of nonsense poems by Walter de la Mare inscribed as having been won by me for 'spoken English' and signed by the Headmaster.

My long school career, four years longer than that of any of the local children, was about to come to an end. I had been allowed to stay so long

CITY OF BIRMINGHAM

WAVERLEY GRAMMAR
SCHOOL

PRIZE

For *Spoken English, Form 1*

Awarded to

Brenda Nash.

F. P. Whiteley
Head Master

July 1951

My first school prize, 1951

at school partly because of my father who had been denied a Grammar School education because his parents had been too poor to buy the necessary books, which made him keen for us to have a good education and partly because I was useful to my mother as nanny, cook and maid of all work, especially in the long summer holidays when the younger children had to be minded while she was at work.

I knew nothing about universities, what they taught, how students were financed, which were good universities or how they worked. I simply chose three universities at random, careful not to pick any too far away for me to be able to raise the money to get there, and applied to them to study French. 'Further education' was to me no more than a meaningless phrase, bandied about at school; what it meant in practice I had no idea. In those days there was no overall body such as UCCA to oversee applications: I simply wrote to Leicester, Nottingham and Sheffield and, in due course, was invited to go to interviews. This, of course, backed me into yet another tight corner, for I had no idea how I was going to raise the money to go so far afield. When I told them when the interviews were my parents nodded absently, but they made no firm promises of money to pay for the trips, so I just waited in a ferment of anxiety as the fateful days approached, trying to prod my parents by timely reminders to offer some kind of financial backing. In the end, the combined efforts of Reggie, Gran and my half-hearted parents raised enough cash for me to take a bus to Nottingham, for my first interview. Having hardly ever been out of Birmingham I always looked upon visits to strange towns with a sense of terror (a fear that has stayed with me all my life), and I was terrified I wouldn't be able to find the university. Ignorant and feeble as I was, however, I did locate the place and was forced to undergo not only a translation test but a long interview conducted all in French, which, on my side at least, was reduced to the briefest monosyllables as replies to the questions put to me. I left the interview as limp as a withered lettuce leaf, in my relief that the ordeal was over, wishing the inquisitors a cheerful 'goodday' in tones so artificially overloud that they startled even me.

Forewarned by this unnerving experience I was more prepared for what was to come in the other interviews and turned my attention again to the problem of raising the money. One cold morning found me at 5am at the bus-stop, waiting for the first bus of the day to take me to the station for a dawn journey to Sheffield. To my amazement, that very early hour was

EXAMINATION SUCCESSES

The following pupils were awarded a General Certificate of Education by the Northern Universities Matriculation Board in July, 1957.

ADVANCED LEVEL

Girls

JEAN ABBISS
ELIZABETH ALLEN
ROSEMARY COOKSON
SHEILA FLANAGAN
JUNE FUDGER
LORNA HAYWOOD
EDNA JONES
LILIA MICHAEL
BRENDA NASH
MARGARET POUNTNEY
ANN STRAIN

Boys

P. ABBOTT
J. ALLEN
E. BRANSON
D. FRANCIS
K. HUMPHRIES
I. JAMES
D. LEES
A. RICHARDS
D. RUDHALL
J. WARD
M. WILLS

ORDINARY LEVEL

Girls

GWENDOLEN AMIES
MARGARET ASHMORE
PAULINE BENNETT
ANNE BENNETT
ANN BILLINGHAM
ANN BOUNDS
ANN BOWDEN
ANN BRADSHAW
PATRICIA BROWN
KATHLEEN BROWN
ANNE BULLOCK
DIANE BUTLER
ANN CARTER
MARJORIE CLARK
JUNE CORBETT
MARGARET CRAY
PAMELA DARNLEY
YVONNE DAVIES
ANN EBBON
MEGAN EDWARDS
PATRICIA EDWARDS
MARJORIE ESSEX
MARGARET FARAGHER
WENDY FISHER
PATRICIA FRECKLETON
BETTY FREEMAN
PAMELA GINIFER
PATRICIA GUEST
MARGARET GUEST
CHRISTINE GYDE
JUNE HALL
SONIA HINSON
RUTH HOWELL

MARGARET HUDSON
ANN HUDSON
JUNE HUNT
WENDY HURST
THELMA JOLLEY
FRANCES JONES
MAUREEN JONES
SYLVIA JOYNSON
PATRICIA LETHERBARROW
ANN LEVASSEUR
JOSEPHINE LOVE
EVELINE MADDOX
MARGARET MERCER
LINDA MCCRACKEN
BERNADETTE MCLAUGHLIN
JACQUELINE NORMAN
JANET PARTINGTON
VERONICA POPE
MIRIAM PRINGLE
ANNE RUDHALL
LORRAINE SOUTHALL
ANN SELWOOD
MARGARET TALBOT
VALERIE TEAGUE
MAUREEN THICKBROOM
GILLIAN TURNER
JEAN WEBB
CYNTHIA WEST
PEGGY WALKER
JEAN WHISKER
AUDREY WILLIAMS
SHEILA YOUNG

My next school prize - 7 years later!

131

peopled by a cheery population, emerging from the dim shadows of a chill winter's morning, cheery greetings cutting the frosty air: "Morning, Charlie. Bit parky this morning!" as the workmen, muffled up in great coats, caps pulled firmly down, caught the early bus to their dawn start. This was a dawn chorus I had known nothing about and it served as a salutary lesson to me about the hard lives so many people led, and I sat in the gloom, half-dozing and half-frozen, listening to the buzz of conversation of the people for whom this hard routine went on every day of the week.

The train journey to Sheffield, through half-glimpsed towns and villages, just coming to life, people stirring and traffic moving, went quickly enough, while I worried about finding the university and not being late for my interview, which was at 9.30. As it happened, all went with a smoothness I'd had no reason to expect: no third degree grilling by a deputation of academics; just a quiet chat with the kindly, avuncular Professor Lawton, who offered me a place in his department almost at once, then despatched me to see the warden of the Woman's Hall of Residence, the aptly-named Miss Bone, the epitome of the prim spinster, hair in a neat bun, carefully toning clothes in suitably restrained colours and a genteel manner. Having been accepted as a suitable resident for her Hall, I made my way somehow back to the station and home.

That left only Leicester. My Gran gave me the money to go there by bus, where I found myself set down in the bus station with absolutely no idea of where the university was. I was not encouraged by asking directions from a couple of people, only to receive a puzzled look and the words, "I didn't know there was a university in Leicester. Are you sure?" Fortunately, the third person I asked not only knew where the university was but was going past it on his way home for lunch and offered to drop me off on the way. The interview itself was not an unqualified success. As a student I was fairly inept: I never read anything outside my set books – I had absolutely no literary background at all; I was indeed depressingly ignorant – 'The Daily Mirror' was the only regular reading in our house, and so I'd never heard of most of the authors I was questioned about. That I was offered a place owed more to the tangible evidence of my 'A' level results than to any spark of intelligence that I might have shown in the interview, but at least, I had been accepted.

Coming out of the university raised for me the spectre of how on earth

I was going to find my way back to the distant bus station. I'd come from there by car and, my sense of direction being as inadequate as it was, I hadn't any clear idea of even in what direction it lay. However, I walked off purposefully down the last road I'd come up into University Road and just walked until, providentially I came upon a young policeman who gallantly escorted me personally the last bit of the way, cheerfully hoping as he left me that he'd see me again when I came up to the university as a student.

I felt a glow of achievement at not only having managed to get to three interviews but also to have been offered places by all three universities. All I had to do now was to choose where I wanted to go. In the end I opted for Leicester as having seemed the most friendly, personal and cosy of the three, more likely to offer the support a feeble, ignorant, nervous person such as myself would no doubt need. I have to admit that my decision was also influenced by the fact that Derek Hogg played football for Leicester City and I looked forward to seeing him play, but with the perversity I had come to expect from life, I found that as soon as I decided to go to Leicester, he was transferred to West Bromwich Albion, where I could have more easily seen him by staying at home!

Having made my decision about which university to go to I then had to put my mind to earning a little money during the summer holiday, to enable me to cope when I went up to university in October. I found myself a little job on the Lode Lane industrial estate in Solihull, a mere bicycle ride from my home, setting stones in costume jewellery. I rode Reggie's bike to work, working from 8am to 5pm. The first week was spent learning how to do the job, instructed by the forewoman, and was paid for this week a flat rate of £5. Once I had become able enough to earn £5 on piecework rates, after the first week, I then was paid at the piecework rate, like the rest of the workers. The pay was hardly generous: white stones (which didn't show the glue if it dripped upon them) were only worth 6d per hundred stones; coloured stones, which showed up carelessly applied glue were paid at a higher rate: 9d per hundred. The glue was very messy and got into everything, sticking your fingers together as you worked and dripping inconveniently into every place it was not meant to be.

Of course, the amount of money you could earn in a week depended upon what jobs you were given to do. A few hundred ear-rings, containing only one stone each and needing to be opened out and placed on a rack to dry, took ages to do and earned you no more than 1/-, and brooches containing many stones of different colours and sizes, for which you had to follow a pattern took equally ages to do and didn't earn much. A few bracelets, each with 100 stones of the same colour and size, however, boosted the earnings no end and ensured that I could earn about £10 a week on average.

Just as I was at home, I was something of a sideshow in the factory. A kindly colleague, Doris, (who is still a friend all these years later) took me under her wing and introduced me to all the customs and rituals of factory work. I was ribbed good-naturedly by my workmates when they found me spending lunch hours, not gossiping out in the sunshine of the back yard, nor exchanging cheeky banter with the men, but reading French classics as a preparation for my university course, but I enjoyed a privileged insight in to the daily lives of so many hard-working people, and was only too well aware of the privilege I was enjoying of an education that would enable me to have what so many of them were denied – choice.

For several weeks I went home at night with fingers stuck together with glue like some web-footed creature of the swamp, hands all grimy and black from the 'antique' jewellery we sometimes set, which was stained with black in an attempt to give it an antique look. Actually, we often used to wonder how on earth the poor souls who actually wore the jewellery got on: if the 'antique' staining came off all over us as we handled it, we dreaded to think what happened to those who actually wore the stuff!

The summer passed and I prepared to go up to university at the beginning of October. I was to be accommodated in a Hall Of Residence, near to the university campus. My father who, by this time, was the proud owner of an old car, drove me to Leicester with my meagre possessions and saw me duly ensconced in my new home. My father had been experimenting for some years with old cars of ancient vintage and sometimes doubtful pedigree. Reggie had started it all, by buying an ancient Austin 7, black with green doors, in the mid-1950s, during the Suez crisis, when learner drivers could drive unsupervised because of petrol rationing, and we'd had great fun careering round the streets, Reggie erratically in control (if that's the right expression), of the vehicle, shaking his fist at motorists who dared to get in his way as he swerved round corners on the wrong side of the road. Actually, he never took a test, and still doesn't drive.

Once Reggie was out of the way in Cyprus, my father decided that something grander than a little Austin 7 was called for, and so began the ongoing process of swapping one heap of old junk for another. First it was a 1934 Rover (which, no doubt, would by now have reached Classic status), a car with a bonnet so long that you had to pull out into the middle of the road at a junction before you could see if any traffic was coming. Having become disillusioned with the Rover, after hurling the driving test examiner into the back, thanks to too efficient brakes and a weak front seat on his driving test, my father then decided on an American car. He'd always secretly fancied himself as a Chicago gangster of the '30s, so he settled on a huge black Packard of gangster-era vintage. It was quite enormous, requiring a tankful of petrol to persuade it to leave the kerbside, but Dad loved the sleek lines and the runningboards, imagining himself, no doubt, standing on one, machine gun in hand, mowing down Al Capone himself! This dream lasted only as long as it took to realise that it was just too thirsty to be a practical proposition, whereupon he swapped it for an equally thirsty Humber Super Snipe, whose flat battery meant that it was imperative that it be parked on a hill, or it would refuse to start.

By the time I left for university in 1958, he had graduated to a blue Standard Vanguard, with quaint divided front windscreen and strangely sloping back, which conveyance bore me to Leicester in the manner to which I was decidedly not accustomed. Here I was, yet again, about to take a leap into the dark.